Le Corps de Latour
COMMEMORATIVE EDITION

BEAULIEU VINEYARD
CENTENNIAL
1900 – 2000

Joel Aiken

JOEL AIKEN

Rod Smith

ROD SMITH

Le Temps de Latour

COMMEMORATIVE EDITION

BEAULIEU VINEYARD
CENTENNIAL
1900 – 2000

ROD SMITH

JOEL AIKEN

BEAULIEU VINEYARD AND THE RISE OF NAPA VALLEY

PRIVATE RESERVE

ROD SMITH

FOREWORD BY
HUGH JOHNSON

PHOTOGRAPHY BY
ANDY KATZ

DAGLAN PRESS
STAMFORD

Contents

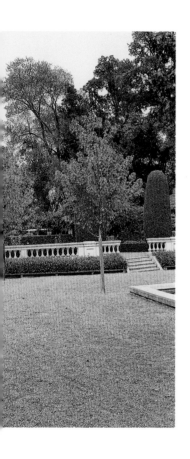

Foreword

When a wine region becomes a legend, a land of treasure peopled by heroes and heroines, it becomes a marketing dream. And marketing is like war: truth is the first casualty. The Napa Valley has not been immune from this risk. It has generated as many reams of mawkish prose as it does all that repetitive back-label stuff for wine wonks. The real lives, struggles and small successes of its inhabitants are all too easily lost in the fog. Until a writer comes along with a story to tell and the wit and nerve to tell it unvarnished.

This is the book you have in your hands: perhaps the most important story in the history of California wine. Its hero is André Tchelistcheff, the diminutive Russian aristocrat who towered over Napa wine when it was still fumbling for quality. Those were times when winemakers worked in huggermugger, afraid to share their experiments with their rivals, when the whole industry was marginal indeed, and prices derisory. André Tchelistcheff's example was strong enough to inspire even people who never met him.

Georges de Latour, founder of Beaulieu Vineyard, successfully established a niche in the nascent Napa wine industry. He made it illustrious by finding and employing a genius. In this book Rod Smith brilliantly explores the chemistry of a relationship that took Napa, and California, giant strides forward.

Beaulieu wines may be less easy to recognize today than they were forty or so years ago. But that is true of virtually every winery, not just in California but round the world. Modern wines are driven by oenological knowledge that our forebears only guessed at. It's the inspired guesswork we remember, while we profit from technical and stylistic advance. Yet, as the story of Beaulieu Vineyard proves, you have to be cussed to make great wine.

Hugh Johnson
Essex, England
10 July 2000

JUST HOW DISTINCTIVE BV WINES WERE IN THE GLORY DAYS OF THE 1950S AND 60S WAS BROUGHT HOME TO ME RECENTLY WHEN CHRISTIAN MOUEIX OF CHÂTEAU PETRUS – NOW OWNER OF DOMINUS IN THE NAPA VALLEY – CAME TO LUNCH WITH US IN THE COUNTRY. I OPENED ONE OF MY FEW REMAINING BOTTLES OF GEORGES DE LATOUR PRIVATE RESERVE CABERNET 1968. CHRISTIAN TOOK ONE SIP AND SAID "I REMEMBER THIS WINE. I HELPED PICK THE GRAPES." IT WAS THE STUDENT-RIOT YEAR. MOUEIX HAD BEEN ARRESTED, THEN GONE UP TO RUTHERFORD TO CALM DOWN, GRAPE-PICKING. AND OVER THIRTY YEARS LATER THE RUTHERFORD DUST WAS STILL IN HIS NOSTRILS. — H.J.

Road to a Legacy

*I*n the spring of 1988, the new owner of a ranch just south of Rutherford, in northern California's Napa Valley, was poking around in a dilapidated shed on the property. The smell of old machine oil permeated the dim enclosure. Wondering what treasures he might stumble upon in the nooks and crannies of his new real estate, the owner assumed that the large object beneath a dust-covered tarpaulin was an antique tractor.

Then he noticed one of the tires peeking out from under the tarp: flat, cracked, and irrevocably mud-stained, it was nonetheless a classic whitewall befitting a luxury roadster of a bygone era.

Pulling the tarp aside, he uncovered a Cadillac Imperial Custom touring car, vintage 1925. The car was covered inside and out with grime, including dark bloodstains that would prove to derive from slaughtered deer; sometime after its heyday, the Cadillac had served an ignoble retirement as a hunting truck. How the touring car came to rest in that shed was never established, but it would not take the new owner long to learn that he now possessed the first-class conveyance once belonging to a legendary figure in the history of American viticulture — Georges de Latour. Fifty years earlier, he had used that very car to bring another great winemaker-to-be from San Francisco to Rutherford, bringing the future of California winemaking right along with them...

"Luis, let's slow down a bit and let Mr. Tchelistcheff enjoy the view. He will be hurried enough when we have set him to work tomorrow." The speaker laughs and his backseat companion echoes him, if uncertainly. Luis, the Portuguese chauffeur who has served Georges de Latour for twenty years, nods decorously and lets up on the grand Cadillac's accelerator, thinking silently that the old man actually wants more time to grill his new employee before they complete their eighty-mile journey from San Francisco to Rutherford.

Normally the boss appreciates Luis's skill in driving fast and safely, for de Latour ordinarily resents the time it takes to get from one place to another when there's business to be done. Usually there is nothing to do but think and gaze out the window. Sometimes he is joined by his wife, Fernande, their son, Richard, and their daughter Hélène with her aristocratic husband, the Marquis de Pins. Otherwise he could spend the time reading or writing, but the roads aren't always paved and not even the Cadillac's lush suspension can make reading and writing comfortable for very long.

On this hot day in September of 1938, the old man has someone new and important to talk to. What are they talking about? Luis can't understand French so he will not be able to pass on gossip for the whole of the Napa Valley to chew on. Nonetheless, speculative versions of the first long talk between de Latour and Tchelistcheff will be passed down for years among the wine folk of Napa, not unlike great bottles of Cabernet.

Both men in the backseat are capable of discourse ranging far beyond their immediate concerns; they share a global viewpoint and a tendency toward strong opinions. Are they discussing native versus imported oak, or the troubling rise of a demagogue in Germany? Luis strains to catch a telltale word or two in English, but can't catch the drift of the conversation. He can tell, at least, that neither of his passengers seems entirely comfortable. Both have a great deal to gain from their new relationship, and even more to lose. Behind their conversation, perhaps each is wondering what he's gotten into.

The owner of the car is a slight man with a large Gallic nose and piercing hazel eyes. A petit bourgeois Frenchman by birth and an American citizen by choice, Georges de Latour is an adventurer, a diplomat, a chemist, a wine producer, and a man of expansive vision — but also a pragmatist. In fact, he is one of the most successful businessmen in the American West. More than three decades ago he founded a Napa Valley wine estate, and could fairly be called America's vintner. Now eighty-two, he will not live to see the time when his wines will be served at state functions celebrating victory in the tremendous war that has just begun in Europe.

Audacious in his younger days, de Latour has grown supremely confident and decisive in his maturity. Having realized recently that his wine production team desperately lacks one key member, he has just gone to Paris and brought that person back with him.

André Tchelistcheff, thirty-seven, is a small man, too, just over five feet tall. His hair is jet-black and his eyes are the color of serpentine. He is a White Russian, born in Moscow near the end of the great age of the Imperial Czars. Tolstoy could have been writing about the Tchelistcheffs in his descriptions of Prince Andrei's family in *War and Peace*. His childhood memories are of hunting wolves with his uncle, riding Orlov horses on his family's estates, following his family's own Tchelistcheff-Borzoi hounds, and huddling with refugees in a crowded, freezing train car rolling

through a blood-drenched Russia at war with itself. As an infantry officer he has led soldiers against machine guns. Yet he is also a brilliant research scientist and an enologist, a direct professional descendant of Louis Pasteur, adept in the young, cutting-edge science of controlled fermentation.

The big saloon car crosses the Napa River, shrunken and muddy at this time of year, and glides up Highway 29 past farms, groves of valley oaks, a long line of monstrous eucalyptus trees planted by pioneers. It passes Napa, a one-time depot and riverfront town that is already outgrowing itself, then Yountville and Oakville, rolling through farms and orchards and, increasingly, vineyards. The Cadillac's passengers roll down their windows, and André gets his first taste of Napa Valley air, which bears the sweet scent of fruit orchards on the rich bottomland between the road and the river.

Approaching Rutherford, the old man tells the driver to slow down even more. That's fine with Luis. He's not above showing off a little, playing up his glamorous image as Mr. de Latour's driver. Later he'll drop into the store at the crossroads for a soda, and everyone will ask about the new arrival. Luis will tell them the man is a very important winemaker from France, a scientist who will make the wines better. But what about Mr. Bonnet, the present winemaker, they will ask? And what about Mr. Ponti, the superintendent, who has run the vineyard and winemaking operations for twenty years? The questions will come thick and fast from the people gathered in the store, with its post office and barbershop. Luis will say he doesn't know any more than that, and they will all nod their heads knowingly. Of course the old man's driver must have heard more than he's telling, but they respect his discretion.

The Cadillac passes the store as it rolls through the little station town. Rutherford is a motley crowd of buildings around the railroad station and the crossroad: Man Sing's little grocery store (the center of a small Chinese community remaining from the Exclusion Act years), and several bars and roadhouses, including the Old Oaken Bucket with one of the valley's earliest wells outside, Tosetti's Mont St. John Bar, and the El Real Café.

Just north of Rutherford the big car glides past a group of men

MAIN STREET,
RUTHERFORD
CALIFORNIA, C.1895

opposite:
GEORGES DE LATOUR,
C.1920

among the vines near the road. One man is talking to some vineyard workers. He's a burly man wearing a wide-brimmed hat against the sun. As the car passes he lifts a hand, and the old man waves back. Luis can't see much of the man's face but a bushy mustache under the wide brim, but he can feel the sharp look directed at the car. Joseph Ponti has been the winery superintendent for more than twenty years. What is he thinking about the arrival of this French enologist?

Luis applies the brakes with a practiced foot and shifts down, at just the right spot on the highway to set the big car into a perfect sweeping turn through the gates of the Beaulieu estate and onto a long tree-lined drive. There in the shade of the big chestnut trees they get out of the car and put their jackets on.

A wide staircase leads to the front door of the big house. An elegant woman awaits them; in contrast to her husband, Madame de Latour is tall and striking, even regal in her bearing. What André Tchelistcheff notices most is her fine, large hat. Many years later he will recall, "It was the most amazing hat I had ever seen — until I saw the one she wore at dinner."

No one is there to photograph it, but nonetheless there is an historic tableau with three distinctive figures: Georges de Latour, who led the young California wine industry to its first worldwide acclaim; Fernande de Latour, who will guide Beaulieu Vineyard through its next quarter-century of standard-setting success; and André Tchelistcheff, whose elegant science-based approach to winemaking will take California wine to the first rank. Leaning against the dusty fender of the Imperial Custom and looking on the scene, Luis senses that he is witnessing a highly significant moment in the still-young story of the fabled Napa Valley.

CHAPTER ONE

In the New World

On a quiet block of Bush Street in San Francisco, at number 825/29, is an ugly square apartment building of steel-reinforced concrete, erected after the 1906 earthquake. It marks the first known U.S. address of a young French chemist named Georges de Latour, the address he gave in 1892 when he filed an affidavit of intent that would lead to his naturalization as an American citizen four years later.

Prior to that there was just one tantalizing reference in the 1892 San Jose City Directory to a temporary residence in a hotel called Lake House, which no longer exists. De Latour is listed there as the proprietor of the California Tartar Works. These are virtually the only documented facts that have emerged about de Latour's early years in California.

At the time of Georges de Latour's death in 1940, several newspaper obituaries stated the questionable claim that he arrived in San Francisco in 1883. In fact, no one knows for sure. There are unsubstantiated accounts in various books and newspapers, including the *St. Helena Star*, that prior to San Francisco he was "interested in mining" in Tuolomne County. One story asserts that he staked, and lost, a small fortune in gold Napoleon coins given to him by his mother. He was also said to have spent some time in Michigan. But we probably will never know exactly when and how de Latour arrived in California.

A PERMANENT DETOUR TO THE NEW WORLD

Georges Marie Joseph de Latour was born on October 20, 1856 in a tiny village called Daglan in southwest France. Daglan is in the Périgord region, near Sarlat and not far from Bordeaux. It's a lush region of deep forest and

dramatic rock formations, punctuated by farms and villages featuring the conical stone silos called *gariottes*. Young Georges grew up among small, diversified farms surrounded by thick woods. The Dordogne Valley comprises a diverse terrain of towering cliffs and sun-dappled glades, flowing water and limestone cliffs — a landscape that evokes the far-distant time when aurochs and mastodons roamed the earth and people lived in caves. Not far from de Latour's boyhood haunts, a pair of youngsters exploring the woods near the village of Lascaux in 1940 would stumble into a cavern with wildly painted walls, discovering a neolithic art site that would change our modern view of the distant past.

The de Latour family was what might be described as landed gentry, but not strictly aristocratic. They grew grapes, among other crops, and lived well. The flavors of foie gras and truffles were part of young Georges's sensory lexicon from an early age. On special occasions the Sunday roast goose was served with a *grand vin* from a château in nearby Bordeaux.

He would doubtless have grown into the life of a gentleman farmer and patriarch but for two tragedies that radically altered his future while he was still a teenager. One was the advent of phylloxera during the 1860s; within a decade the tiny root-sucking aphid had devastated every western European wine region of note. The de Latours lost their vines, too, and with the lucrative grape crop went much of the family fortune.

The other loss was more harrowing: the death of his parents, apparently from disease. He was taken in by family friends in Sarlat. M. and Mme de Boisson saw to his further upbringing and education.

For all his tribulations Georges de Latour was well educated, indeed. He received a solid basic education at a local school in Sarlat, then a good liberal arts grounding at the École Centrale in Paris. Many years after his death a longtime family friend and trusted employee, Joseph Ponti, stated in an interview that de Latour had talked about attending a Catholic college in London. According to this story he had intended to become a priest before reluctantly accepting the fact that he hadn't really heard the call. De Latour's granddaughter, Mrs. Walter Sullivan, disputes the story, stating emphatically that de Latour did not go to school in London and never studied for the priesthood. She agrees, however, that he studied chemistry and became a good practical chemist.

In any case, young Georges was qualified for any number of positions in the world, including business management. In a precocious display of the adventuresome spirit that played such a big role in his later success, he decided to leave France and seek his fortune in the New World.

The late nineteenth century was a time when technology and capital had caught up with natural resources. Fortunes were being made by bold entrepreneurs in the American West, South America, Australia, and Canada. At that time there were mining booms in Chile and Peru, cattle bonanzas in Argentina, Canada, and the United States, and rushes for gold, silver, and gems on the Orinoco and other South American jungle rivers. Some of the adventurers had even recognized the need for fine New World wines and were establishing vineyards and wineries in Chile's coastal valleys and the Andean foothills of Argentina.

Georges had an uncle living in South America. Resolving to go there and live with his uncle while trying the business climate, he purchased a one-way steamship ticket to Rio de Janeiro. On the eve of departure he was notified that his uncle in Latin America had died. It's hard to understand why he didn't board the ship anyway. No doubt he had already demonstrated his enterprise and reliability, so it's reasonable to assume that he might have been entrusted with some of his uncle's affairs. Perhaps there was also news of financial difficulties; his uncle might have had debts or liens that his nephew would have inherited. At any rate, once Georges committed himself to striking out for the New World but no longer had a concrete reason for going to South America, he found himself attracted to North America instead. There is a striking parallel here with André Tchelistcheff's dilemma some sixty years later. Like de Latour, Tchelistcheff would be on the verge of going to South America, then suddenly change his mind to choose California.

THE WILD WEST
IN FERMENT

*D*id Georges de Latour go to the Sierra Nevada goldfields before settling in San Francisco? Historians have searched for some evidence of that to no avail. In any case, he arrived in the United States in the midst of a sudden, deep economic recession, the first since before the Civil War. At that time a dozen of the present states had not yet been admitted to the union. A savage civil war and its turbulent aftermath had radically altered the eastern seaboard, and the states of the former Confederate States of America had just begun to redeem their places in the U.S. government.

CHARDONNAY GRAPE CLUSTER FORMING BETWEEN BLOOM AND SET

The West was up for grabs. The native tribes, devastated by European-borne diseases and dogged by hunter-killer U.S. Army units, made their last futile stand on the high plains. The Battle of Little Bighorn in 1870 marked the beginning of their end. In the same year Congress passed the Homestead Act, which opened vast lands to settlement. So even as the sun was setting on the native North American tribal nations, millions of white Americans, a large proportion of them immigrants from Europe, were pouring across the Mississippi River and heading west.

Most of California in the 1870s and 80s was still a frontier, although international ocean trade gave San Francisco and the surrounding region an unusual degree of cosmopolitan sophistication. It was little more than two decades since John Sutter's discovery of a shiny pebble in the American River had set off one of the largest gold rushes in history, creating a large and diverse population virtually overnight. California had become a state in 1850, and in 1869 the transcontinental railroad was completed with the driving of a golden spike in Promontory, Utah. The railroad transformed the western continent in striking ways. Whistle-stops grew into towns, usually for natural and logical reasons but sometimes at random. Some of the important towns became cities, and some of those became commercial centers, then territorial loci with federal offices and eventually, state capitals. Expansion created a matrix of dynamic but unpredictable regional economies whose fluctuations were already being felt in Europe.

The new railroad system was a moving population center, a steel-rail overland echo of the Mississippi and its tributaries. It was a world in motion, like a river system with many eddies, and each eddy had its own particular personality. Stockyard towns tended to be party districts with robust red-light enterprises that gave international criminal elements their first footholds in America. Outside the narrow population corridors following the rail lines, the land was so wild that you could be reasonably sure of attracting unwanted attention if you were foolish enough to light a campfire on raised ground.

California was part of this frontier, and yet apart. It was not the kind of frontier where settlers competed with natives and nature for survival. In the most desirable areas, including northern California, the land had been settled early on. In fact it was rather crowded around Los Angeles and San Francisco by the time Georges de Latour arrived in the West.

DISCOVERING
A NATIVE COMMODITY

*I*t wasn't so much land that was up for grabs in California, but new wealth of all kinds. There were fortunes to be made by entrepreneurs, and there were plenty of wildcat businessmen on hand to try their various skills and knowledge in pursuit of the dollar. Georges de Latour was one of those people.

He took his time getting to California, landing first in New York and spending some time in Michigan on his way. In the beginning he got by any way he could — picking cherries in the San Joaquin Valley, acting as a doctor in San Francisco. That was a pattern he would follow in later years, except that "getting by" would mean starting and running his own businesses rather than merely being employed by others.

We do know that Georges de Latour became a naturalized American citizen in 1896, in San Francisco. At that time he registered to vote and listed his residence as 829 Bush Street. In the late 1880s he hooked up with a fellow Frenchman named de Guigné and entered the cream of tartar business, as a purchaser of raw materials for the Wheeler, Reynolds & Stauffer Chemical Company. By 1896 he was listed in the San Francisco Directory as a director of Stauffer. During the same period, apparently, he started his own company, the California Tartar Works, based in San Jose with satellite plants in Healdsburg and Napa.

Cream of tartar, a primary material in commercial baking, is made from crystallized double potassium tartrates, or argols. One excellent source of argols was the inside of wine fermentation vessels. Dense tartaric acid deposits formed on the walls of the tanks, and were "harvested" by going into the tank with a hatchet and chopping away the crust, then breaking it up further and bagging it in 100-pound sacks. A single visit to a fairly large winery with several fermentation tanks could be quite profitable, and the resource was renewed after every vintage.

An 1898 article in the *San Francisco Call* described the industry: "The business of producing cream of tartar and tartaric acid exists in the United States only in California…. Tartaric acid is resident in many vegetables, chief among which is the grape. All that scum, which rising upon the surface of the wine by the fermenting of the fluid, gathers upon the sides of the casks, is exceedingly rich in the acid, containing sometimes as high as forty percent of that chemical." The article goes on to report that California produced about half a million pounds of cream of tartar annually at around $.20/pound, making the industry worth about $100,000 a year.

Georges de Latour contracted with virtually every large winery in northern California for tartaric acid residues. He drove around the wine country in a carriage to inspect and buy the argols. One of his assistants later recalled that de Latour was not above entering a tank with hammer and chisel to hack out the crystals himself. By 1897 he was concentrating primarily on his own company while still a director of Stauffer, which appears to have been the sole buyer of argols from the American Cream of Tartar Association — which meant he was serving on the board of his only customer.

Later, the processing plants he built in Healdsburg, San Jose, Napa, Fresno, and (after moving to Rutherford) at Beaulieu allowed him to bypass much of the laborious and inefficient method of going into individual tanks to chop out the argols. Now, he could buy the pomace from the wineries, put it into large tanks, and heat the tanks with steam. Subsequently cooling the tanks precipitated the tartrate crystals, which were then dried in the sun on large sheets of canvas before being bagged.

This method had an added benefit: once the argols were extracted, the pomace could be distilled into brandy. So Georges de Latour had figured out how to profit twice from a single purchase of material, an early example of his uncommon and sometimes crafty style of enterprise.

STAKING A CLAIM
IN THE WINE COUNTRY

At the same time, the cream of tartar business had its challenges: in 1897, de Latour was sued by residential neighbors of his San Jose plant over the strong odors emanating from the building, and was forced to close the plant. The following year, lowered tariffs on French tartrate exports virtually closed the eastern U.S. market to California producers, drastically cutting profits.

In one other respect, the entrepreneur's time at Stauffer was vital. In the office there was a lovely young stenographer who caught his eye. She had large, commanding ice-blue eyes and she dressed impeccably. She was Fernande Romer, the daughter of a German immigrant who had been a judge in Berlin. Fernande had been born in Alsace-Lorraine in 1875, just after the war between Germany and France during which that area was annexed by Germany. When she was still little the Romers came to San Francisco and opened a small hotel, but shortly thereafter her father died, and her mother moved the family (Fernande, her two sisters and a brother) to Vallejo. Georges and Fernande were married on April 25, 1898, in the Church of Notre Dame des Victoires at 566 Bush Street in San Francisco.

The de Latours then settled in the little northern Sonoma County wine town of Healdsburg, in the big bend of the Russian River where it begins its westward run from Alexander Valley to the sea, and where one of the Association's processing factories was located. They purchased a large house next to the Giuseppe Simi family, which owned Simi Winery. Georges and Giuseppe became good friends. When Georges installed an electrical generator in his house, an impressive technological innovation at the time, he also wired the Simi house. For a while, these two were the only houses in Healdsburg with electricity. While the de Latours were living in Healdsburg their first child, Richard, was born.

Perhaps it was mere happenstance that the enterprising immigrant got his start by locating a regional commodity to trade. That Georges chose cream of tartar, a wine industry byproduct, may have been a simple coincidence — he was, after all, a trained chemist in search of opportunity — yet it looks suspiciously like forethought. Purchasing argols gave him a perfect opportunity to get to know the wine country and put him in direct contact with all the important wine producers. After years of personally studying the lay of the land, he established his own wine estate in the heart of the Napa Valley, one of the finest viticultural locations in California. Was the whole argols venture designed as a scouting mission?

We can only speculate. All we really know is this: From his very first successful commercial venture, Georges de Latour set a brilliant and virtually unerring course toward the new world of American wine.

CHAPTER TWO

The Century Turns

Whether they intended it that way or not, the time Georges and Fernande de Latour spent in the northern California wine country prepared them well for the venture on which they would stake everything. Their familiarity with grape growing areas led them to establish the heart of the Beaulieu empire in Rutherford, at the very heart of the Napa Valley — an area that would subsequently prove to be one of California's finest viticultural enclaves.

As he drove along the wine country roads, first driving his own wagon but soon riding in a carriage (he liked having a driver, even then), Georges de Latour cast a keen eye on the landscape, noting which properties appeared to be thriving and which looked run-down and possibly for sale.

At first he was strongly attracted to the Sonoma side of the Mayacamas Range. He had missed the initial window of opportunity in the lower Sonoma Valley, which was already in the hands of descendants of General Vallejo and Agostin Haraszthy. But farther north, toward Glen Ellen, where the Kohler-Froeling winery produced large quantities of wine for sale in bulk, there were some promising enclaves. A brash young writer named Jack London would shortly stake his claim there, infusing the local culture with his personality through the next century. Santa Rosa was already a center of commerce, service, and finance, a quickly-growing city not unlike Napa, though without the access by water. Still, the region was commercially and politically uncertain — the currents and eddies of fortune were undefined, and it was hard to tell which direction things would go.

To the west, the Russian River Valley was a daunting wilderness where vineyards were carved out of the forest with great effort, only to be at the mercy of the sea fog that could keep a good crop of grapes from ripening fully in some years. Healdsburg, where the de Latours lived for a time, was more amenable. There were already substantial wine cultures in Dry Creek Valley and Alexander Valley by the 1880s, and he knew his way around. Yes, Healdsburg was a possibility.

Yet the more time he spent in the crescent-shaped valley to the east of the Mayacamas, the more he liked it. Napa Valley had quickly become the most wine-oriented area of northern California, thanks to an influx of Europeans during the 1870s. Even Charles Krug, cellarmaster at Haraszthy's Buena Vista Winery in Sonoma, had gone over the mountains to Napa when he struck out on his own. A coalition of Napa vintners had founded a bank and helped fund a railroad that was dedicated less to passengers than to transporting the valley's principal crops — prunes, fruit, and wine. Where the Healdsburg area had a sense of isolation, Napa felt connected with the world of global business. He often took the steamship from San Francisco to Vallejo and then rode the train up and down the valley, stopping to do business at wineries along the way. Most of all, the landscape appealed to him.

SINKING ROOTS
IN GOOD SOIL

*R*iding along the rails or the well-maintained dirt road that ran next to them, skirting the Mayacamas foothills, de Latour could feel the superb balance of the climate. Often while making his rounds by carriage he would stop to stretch his legs and pick up handfuls of dirt. He liked the way it smelled and the way it crumbled slowly through his fingers in clean little chunks. It was dense and light at the same time, a fine combination of clay, sand, and gravel that would support the vines without encouraging them too much. From his earliest youth in Périgord it had been drummed into Georges's head that grapevines needed to be somewhat stressed to produce good wine. This well-drained benchland soil between the Napa River and the forested slopes would stress the vines enough to build character without being so cruel that they produced mean wines.

To his mind, the area around Rutherford, at the valley's heart, was the golden spot for vineyards. Because of the wineries already concentrated there, he often got off the train at Rutherford or St. Helena and hired a carriage for several days while he did business with the winery owners. He got to know the vintners and other people who worked the land. His familiarity with the Bordeaux region told him that the best Napa wineries were pursuing an international standard. These vintners were looking less to local markets than toward San Francisco and New York, and beyond to the more refined world across the Atlantic Ocean. This contrasted with the parochial attitude of the wine community to the west in Sonoma County.

Throughout the summer and fall of 1899, Georges de Latour found himself looking forward to driving past a particular stretch of the Napa Valley road just north of Rutherford. West of the road, on rising land dotted with ancient oak trees, was a small "ranch" (the Californian word for farm) with a stream running through it. There was a little knoll and at its base a white

two-story Victorian house surrounded by palm trees, a small cottage, and a cavernous three-story barn/stable. Much of the property was planted with fruit trees, and the rest was in hay. It was a pretty place, not as grandly developed as the adjoining Inglenook estate, with its great stone winery and Captain Gustav Niebaum's fine wooden house, but idyllic nonetheless. He asked around and learned that the place was for sale.

The ranch was owned by Charles P. Thompson, a member of the second-wave pioneer family which had made the river bottom south of Napa bloom with fruit orchards in the 1870s — for them, a literal case of money growing on trees. But this ranch appeared to be a little run-down. Moreover, there was a small vineyard and the adjoining terrain promised a fruitful expansion.

It looked like a good place to establish a wine estate. However, the $12,000 price tag was steep, even in 1900. De Latour turned to an old friend for advice. John Wheeler had worked with him at the Stauffer Chemical Company, and left at about the same time. Now he was living in Napa Valley, in a stone house that he built just north of Rutherford, with his own winery next door. De Latour recalled years later how he asked Wheeler for advice in the matter:

> "John, I have a chance to buy the Thompson place," said de Latour to his old friend. "I don't have a lot of money. What do you think?"
>
> "It is a lot of money," Wheeler agreed. "But Georges, that's one of the best locations in the valley. If you buy it, you'll never be sorry."

Fernande agreed. She had fallen in love with the property immediately. She began to refer to it as *beaulieu,* "beautiful place." They promptly sold the cream of tartar processing plant in Healdsburg to the French-American Company, and used the money to purchase the Thompson place in May, 1900. Because de Latour was already known in the northern California wine world, the purchase was noted in the *St. Helena Star* on May 18:

> "G. de Latour, of San Francisco, manager of the California Tartar company, has purchased the splendid home of Charles Thompson, near Rutherford, the transaction having been closed Saturday.
>
> "The sale was made by the W.A. Mackinder Co. The place is comprised of one to five acres of fertile soil improved with a fine two-story house and convenient outbuildings.
>
> "It is partly planted to orchard and the remainder is sown each year for hay

THE BEAULIEU ESTATE AND GARDENS WITH BV#1, THE FIRST VINEYARD PLANTED BY GEORGES DE LATOUR, IN THE BACKGROUND

or grain. The orchard is one of the finest in the Valley and the farm shows the care it has received during the thirty years it has been the property of Mr. Thompson.

"G. de Latour, the purchaser, will take possession June 1, and will immediately inaugurate extensive improvements. He will have painters at work painting, papering, and tinting, and will renovate the house from top to bottom.

"The most important feature of the purchase, however, is that Mr. de Latour will, it is expected within a month, commence the erection of a cream of tartar factory which, when in operation, will furnish employment for a large number of hands. Connected with his plant will also be a fruit drying establishment. For these purposes, four acres of land near the railroad track have been reserved. The entire place not in orchard, will be planted to resistant vineyard. These changes and the enterprises which will be launched not only means much to Rutherford but to the entire Napa Valley.

"Mr. de Latour and family will spend the summer months at their new country home. They expect to be there this season until November."

The de Latours had stepped up to a new level of enterprise — now they needed capital. Accordingly, they incorporated the California Tartar Works in 1901, as a prelude to selling the majority of shares to the Stauffer Chemical Company, of which Georges was still a director. Shortly thereafter they purchased 127 contiguous acres from Charles Thompson and planted their first vineyard, about eighty acres of Zinfandel and Petite Sirah vines. The vineyard would henceforth be known as the Home Ranch, or BV#1.

They sold their first crop of grapes three years later. But the year 1904 was more significant for several other events: Their second child, Hélène, was born in San Jose (so they must have still been spending time there). Then their house burned down. According to family tradition, they were all going on a trip, and there were several large wardrobe-style steamer trunks. Young Richard set a candle on one of them and it fell over, setting the trunk and then the house on fire. Almost immediately, the family began building a new, larger house on the other side of the stream. Time was of the essence; there was neither time nor money to hire an architect. As Fernande de Latour often said later, the house had "a Queen Anne front and a Mary Anne back."

The year 1904 also saw the birth of the commercial entity called Beaulieu Vineyard.

A FALSE START FOR
A NEW INDUSTRY

By the time the de Latours arrived in Napa Valley, the California wine industry was on the downside of its first boom. That had been done in by phylloxera, recession, and poor winemaking. But it didn't take a visionary to see the valley's potential, which meant that the cycle would tend upward again. Meanwhile, it was a good time to buy land.

The northern California wine community at the turn of the century was the flowering of a subculture that had started more than a hundred years earlier. Its heartbeat was strongest in the foothills of the Mayacamas Range, on both the east and west flanks: in the Valley of the Moon and in Napa Valley. The business environment was insular; a dollar might go around and around, passing through a lot of the same households and businesses any number of times before passing out of the wine community.

California's first wines were made by Franciscan monks during the Spanish occupation in the late eighteenth century. Wines were produced at several of the twenty one missions along the track known as El Camino Real from San Diego to Sonoma. Those mission grapes were an obscure Mediterranean *Vitis vinifera* variety called Criolla. By all accounts the early mission wines were dull and undistinguished, tending toward sweetness but also quite tannic, low in acid and high in alcohol. The few modern examples of Criolla produced by California wineries from descendants of those early vines (just a few hundred acres statewide in 1999) generally match that description, despite being made with all the consideration accorded the so-called noble grapes. In other words, we can now taste the best possible rendition of the Criolla without being impressed. The early wines were good enough to cheer the fathers and the soldiers, and reportedly helped make the natives more amenable to "conversion" or enslavement.

In 1822 the Spanish flag was replaced by the eagle and snake of the newly independent republic of United Mexican States. It was during the

Mexican period that the mission system declined, opening the way for entrepreneurial wine production. The first commercial vineyard operation on record was near the Pueblo de los Angeles. In 1833 a Frenchman named Louis Vignes established a vineyard he called El Aliso Rancho; the site of that historic planting now lies under pavement in the heart of what is now the largest city in the United States, near Los Angeles's Union Station.

Vignes is known to have imported the first non-mission grape varieties from Europe. There is no record of what they were, but because he hailed from the village of Cadillac in Bordeaux (not far from the village near Périgord where Georges de Latour was born), they may have been Bordelais varieties such as Cabernet, Malbec, and Carmenier, all of which appeared in Chile at about the same time. Vignes went out of business after a few years, and although he must have supplied cuttings to some of the other grape growers in the Los Angeles area, the mission remained the grape variety of choice in southern California. At any rate, the point had been made that fine wine could be produced in California.

By the time Commodore Sloat raised the American flag over Monterey on July 7, 1847, vineyards were well-established in Alta California. A month before the American Annexation, the famous Bear Flag was raised in

Sonoma Plaza by a group of rebels that included several Napans, including members of the nascent wine community.

California became a state in 1850, and two years later the state capital was moved from Monterey to Sacramento. There were a lot of connections between Napa and Sacramento. Some were governmental associations that simply transferred from Monterey with the change. At the same time, the shift tended to magnify and reinforce existing relations. With Sacramento a day's ride away, Napans began spending more time in political circles than their formerly influential southern California counterparts.

In many ways, the story of nineteenth century Napa Valley wine reads like an early script for the wine boom of the late twentieth century. Overall, it was a false start on a rather grand scale. The early success of some producers indicated what was theoretically possible, and that was followed by a vigorous influx of passion-driven capital and the subsequent loss of much of that capital as a result of vine disease, economic turbulence, and increasingly dominant competition. It didn't help that California producers in general hurt their own cause during the boom years by shipping poor wine back East, where it was soundly trounced in the marketplace by sound if undistinguished French *vins de pays*.

Serious Napa Valley wine production began in 1858 when St. Helena pioneer John Patchett hired an intense young Prussian immigrant named Charles Krug to produce wine from his St. Helena estate (about 2,000 gallons of mission red, using a wooden cider press). Krug was an erstwhile revolutionary and political fugitive from Germany who had learned his winemaking in Sonoma, where he worked for Agostin Haraszthy at Buena Vista. The well-educated young man, with his neatly-trimmed beard and spectacles, was easily accepted by the wealthier immigrants and became the valley's first high-profile winemaking consultant, foreshadowing the modern crew of well-paid winemakers who produce most of the modern cult or "lifestyle" wines in Napa. Krug made wine for several wealthy Napans, including George Yount, before establishing his own winery, with twenty-three acres of mission grapes, near St. Helena in 1861; his place as winemaker to the wealthy was assumed by his Swiss assistant, Henry Pellet.

The will was there, the basic wine knowledge was there, the momentum was there. Everything was in place — almost. The only thing between Napa Valley and fine wine was the mission grape.

TOWARD A FINER VINE

Anyone familiar with fine European wines would have recognized right away that while a good winemaker can coax decent wine from mission grapes, the potential for great wine simply isn't there. That was apparent early on to Agostin Haraszthy, who is credited with importing the first large quantities of diverse European vine cuttings to California. It was also obvious to a good friend of Haraszthy's, Dr. George Belden Crane, who settled in St. Helena in 1859.

Crane not only planted European varieties, he installed his vineyard on the dry, gravelly benchland between the soil-thin foothills and the heavy valley floor clay. His neighbors shook their heads and laughed at his folly. Following his first crush in 1862, those who knew anything about wine realized that Crane was on the right track. Although the mission continued to dominate Napa Valley viticulture through the 1890s on the strength of its high yield and easy vinification, the cutting edge of Napa Valley's ultimate

success began in Dr. Crane's site-variety matching experiments in his St. Helena vineyard. (He donated the property to the town on his death and it became the grounds of St. Helena High School; like Vignes's El Aliso Ranch, that historic vineyard site now lies under pavement.)

BV#1, LOOKING EAST,
A FEW YEARS AFTER
THE FIRST PLANTING,
C.1917

Dozens of German, Swiss, and French immigrants found their ways to the Napa Valley in the 1870s, founding many of the valley's first wave of wineries. By 1880 there were nearly two dozen wineries between Oakville and St. Helena. Among the most prominent were the Ewer-Atkinson Winery in Rutherford, owned by former California Senator Seneca Ewer in partnership with the Atkinson family, and Swiss immigrant John Thomann's winery at Vineland Station, just south of St. Helena. The Frenchmen Jean Chaix and Jean Brun founded the Nouveau Médoc Winery in Rutherford, across the County Road from the Ewer Winery. A Finnish sea captain named Gustav Niebaum developed a majestic wine estate he called Inglenook in Rutherford. Other high-profile vintners included H.W. Crabb, who called his property To Kalon. North of St. Helena were the "three Jakes," Grimm, Schram, and Beringer. Jacob Beringer planted trees along the county road that passed in front of their Los Hermanos estate; those trees form a majestic tunnel over Main Street north of town. Several of the new wineries, including Ewer's, were designed by Hamden McIntyre, an engineer and architect who also

served as the first general manager of the Inglenook estate.

Not all of the newcomers followed Dr. Crane's lead toward the finer *Vitis vinifera* grapes. Even among the ones who did, the potential was often lost to unsanitary winemaking conditions. Prof. George Hussman, a member of the California Agricultural Commission in the 1880s, complained that "I have often been in wineries that looked more like slaughterhouses, with the purple juice bubbling over the top, a crust a foot thick had formed on top, which had become dry and moldy, was swarming with vinegar flies, and in many cases, maggots were crawling around lively. When the fermentation was over, the whole mass was often left for a week yet, as the manipulator thought to gain for it color and tannin, and become more saleable thereby. That under such treatment decomposition and acidification had set in, can hardly surprise anyone."

Maggots or no, the wine industry pressed on with mounting success. Louis Pasteur's investigations in how to control spoilage organisms was not lost on such early vintners as Gustav Neibaum, whose sanitation practices in the Inglenook winery were scrupulous. Niebaum also made an early commitment to finer grapes than the mission — although his affection for the Black Malvoisie was perhaps misplaced.

The pride of place which characterizes Napa Valley today was not apparent in those days. Early on it became the accepted norm to label wines generically with the names of European regions. This was meant to be a stylistic distinction, but more often masked a multitude of confusions as to what the given wine was supposed to be. Burgundy, for example, seldom contained any Pinot Noir, the sole red grape of Burgundy. It was simply a red wine blended from any and all grapes, including Cabernet Sauvignon. Likewise Claret, which was meant to emulate Bordeaux but which seldom did.

Nonetheless, the consolidated foundation of a long-thriving wine industry seemed secure when several prominent wine producers united to establish a bank with the intention of providing financial services and resources to the burgeoning wine community. The Bank of St. Helena was founded in

1882 by eleven vintners, including Seneca Ewer, Charles Krug, H.W. Crabb, John Thomann, and Gustav Niebaum. It eventually spun off a marketing organization, the Napa Valley Wine Company, which might be regarded as a precursor to the Napa Valley Vintners Association established in 1942. The Napa Valley Wine Company was so successful that within a few years it had become the California Wine Association, operating bulk wineries in Napa and Sonoma.

Meanwhile, the forces driving toward a massive social experiment called Prohibition were already underway. An 1885 ballot proposal that would have made Napa County dry failed by just seven votes.

THE CHARACTER OF AN EMERGING WINEMAKER

Into the small but vigorous world of Napa Valley entrepreneurs came Georges de Latour in the 1880s. He entered the wine-producing community gradually, getting to know the vintners first through his tartrate contracts. Eventually, he joined their ranks.

He was unquestionably a dynamic man. He seems to have been universally admired and respected, if not always liked. Words like stubborn, volatile and unpredictable come up in recollections of Georges de Latour, although not nearly as often as shrewd. He didn't necessarily want to do the best thing over the profitable thing. For example, although he acquired vineyards and plantable land with passion, almost with lust, he had to be convinced to upgrade the quality of the winery. And it took a lot of convincing. But when he finally decided that it was the right decision, he took the visionary step of going outside the local sphere to the highest international standard, thus introducing a French-trained winemaker who would transform the California wine industry. That's the way he saw himself and his business: on the international level, rather than just in the context of a paradisaical little coastal valley that bore more than a little resemblance to the wine estates outside Rome in the first century.

De Latour was well-educated, read Latin and Greek, and was fond of quoting from the classics. As a more-than-fierce competitor, he might well have addressed his rivals using Cicero's words to conspirators in the Roman

Senate two thousand years earlier: "You do nothing, you plan nothing, you think of nothing which I not only do not hear, but which I do not see and know every particular of."

On the other hand, this *homme des affaires* was overwhelmingly remembered by people who knew him on a personal level in glowing terms such as charming, witty, entertaining and engaging. Perhaps fortunately, we know nothing of any vices (unless we classify his fondness for strong tobacco as a vice), nor whether he had a dark side. Even a generation away from a life that was more public than most, we have already lost big pieces of the picture of his complete personality. Georges de Latour was a person more referred to than quoted, and he wasn't quoted much at all. In today's glamour-hungry world, people like Georges and Fernande de Latour would be media royals.

De Latour seems to have had an almost mystical acumen in business — a combination of imagination and practicality behind the attitude of an imperial wildcat. Especially in the scramble to get established during the early years, and in the incredible change of fortune during the Volstead era of Prohibition, we see a risk-taker who's careful not to bite off too much yet also enjoys a good personal challenge.

He also appears to have been extremely benevolent. At least, it could look that way based on his close association with the Catholic Church and his apparent effort to pull as many of his fellow vintners as possible along with him through the ordeals of phylloxera and Prohibition. One of the most compelling aspects of the entire Georges de Latour story is that every one of his benevolent acts ended up making him richer. Indeed, to the long list of Georges de Latour's virtues we can certainly add good timing.

By all accounts, this emerging winemaker was easy to get along with — all the more for people outside the business. He was gracious, the consummate gentleman, ready to listen and to praise and to cap the conversation with a witty remark. And then he forgot all about you.

If he respected you and valued your opinion, however, you were in for a kind of ongoing battle. He expected those in his inner circle to express their views honestly and be ready to back them up. It was his management style as well as in personal life. He handpicked his associates and confidants as much for their temperament as their abilities. He would argue, cross-examine, consider, and then make his decision.

That started with his wife. Fernande de Latour was a woman to be reckoned with, and her husband was the one who had to reckon with her first and most often. Although Georges was the boss, family and close friends witnessed passionate and closely-reasoned arguments about how things ought to be done.

Of course, Fernande never second-guessed or contradicted Georges publicly. That was good, because she did much of the talking, at least in public. As the syndicated Scripps-Howard columnist Ernie Pyle observed after a visit to Beaulieu in 1939, Georges was "a rabidly loyal American. Yet his French is still so strong that a stranger can hardly follow him." A terrific team, especially in social situations, Georges and Fernande were able to work a room like a matched pair of sheepdogs, and they used that ability to good effect. Time and again, when the business encountered some kind of political or bureaucratic obstacle, the de Latours would invite the appropriate officials to dinner and the problems would get ironed out. As their granddaughter Dagmar put it, "They'd invite the supervisors to a big bang-up meal, and get a lot of things they might not have gotten otherwise."

He had great respect for his superintendent, Joseph Ponti, so of course they disagreed frequently. It was fairly common to see Georges de Latour stomp away from Ponti, speed off in his Cadillac, then return a half hour later to continue the discussion. Negotiations often took place in Ponti's truck. Georges would tell his chauffeur to wait, get into Ponti's truck, and they'd drive off. After awhile the truck would come back and the two men would be chatting and laughing together, and Georges would get back into the Cadillac and go home.

On summer afternoons at Beaulieu, as the day's heat gave way to soft twilight and the breezes flowing down the Mayacamas ravines perfumed the air, he often went for walks with his granddaughter, Dagmar de Pins. An early victim of polio who was unable to walk through her mid-teens, Dagmar sat in her wheelchair while Georges rolled her along the paths in the gardens and beneath the trees along the stream bank. She remembers that he told good stories, that he listened to what she had to say, and that he often quoted Racine and Molière.

THE BIRTH OF BEAULIEU

The company that was formally titled Beaulieu Vineyard, San Francisco was incorporated on April 6, 1904. The first stockholders' meeting, on April 10, was attended by directors Jerome H. Kann, William Maxwell, John O'Connor, T.J. Crowley, and J.L. Hanna. Significantly, Crowley and Hanna, and possibly O'Connor, were Catholic priests; Hanna would soon become Archbishop. At the next board meeting, one week later, Georges de Latour and Fernande de Latour were named to the Board of Directors, along with J.C. Lloyd, who was named vice president. Directors Hanna, O'Connor, and Maxwell resigned from the board at that time.

Meanwhile, the big old barn on the ranch became a wine storage facility, partitioned with a space designated to hold about two dozen barrels of wine. The de Latours had no grapes or winemaking equipment as yet, so they purchased wine from other producers. In the beginning the wine was an off-dry white called Sauterne that was made by the Wente Winery in Livermore. Those early deals marked the beginning of a relationship that would later prove vital to both parties.

By the end of the month, the de Latours had sold their 128 acres of vineyard land to the company in exchange for stock. The property was valued

at $26,000, or about $203 per acre — a basic price of $10,000 over and above the $15,000 mortgage on the property (held by the San Francisco banking firm Donohoe-Kelly), plus a $1,000 debt to a Catholic priest named de Conninck. Georges de Latour received 498 shares of stock (out of a total 500 shares) in return for the vineyard.

At this same meeting, the position of General Manager was created, with the stipulation that this officer would live on the corporation's property. Georges de Latour was appointed General Manager. In his first official address to the board, de Latour promised that the vineyard would begin paying for itself with its first crop of grapes in the coming harvest.

On September 2, 1904, Georges de Latour was named president of Beaulieu Vineyard Corporation. His salary was $100 a month. (Fifteen years later, on the eve of Prohibition, his salary would be a little more than $1,600 a month, or $20,000 a year.)

That fall, the BV Corporation leased the idle John Thomann winery, between Rutherford and St. Helena at Vineland Station, just one stop north of BV. De Latour made some 12,000 gallons of wine. Some was for the church, but much of it was meant for distillation. The next year, however, the corporation sold its grapes to the California Wine Association for $22 a ton. The contract with the CWA was renewed annually for the next three years, and in 1908 the corporation entered a twenty year contract to sell grapes to the CWA.

While the grapes were making money, however, the de Latours commenced making their own wines in 1909. These early wines were not made from their own grapes, but rather from grapes that were purchased or grown under lease, primarily from the 146-acre Henry Jerome vineyard which they leased, with an option to buy, in 1909. For two years the wines were made in a leased facility while the stable on the home ranch was outfitted for vinification; the first wines were made on the estate in 1911.

The minute-books of board meetings during those years show that the company's finances were managed on an event-to-event basis. A few barrels of wine would be purchased and sold, then more wine purchased and sold, and so on. Immediate expenses were often met by procuring loans in various ways, such as borrowing money against future grape crops. Sometimes Georges and Fernande lived virtually hand-to-mouth. Georges did what he could, and what he had to do. For two years he operated a retail wine cellar, the Golden State Wine Company, in San Francisco. He reportedly worked as a pharmacist, or possibly a physician, in the Gold Rush country, and even picked cherries in the San Joaquin Valley. Several times he was sued by creditors, but by all accounts managed to pay back every penny he borrowed, with interest.

Not yet a success by any means, Georges de Latour was nonetheless in his element. He had come to the United States of America because it was a democracy and, in business, a real meritocracy — a fabled land of opportunity. Ironically, democracy itself would provide his biggest challenge, in the form of a puritanical movement that he would characteristically turn to his advantage. But before meeting the challenge called Prohibition there was something more dire and insidious to be dealt with — something creeping in the very soil upon which Georges de Latour hoped to build his fortune.

PAINTED PORTRAIT OF
FERNANDE DE LATOUR,
C.1925

CHAPTER THREE

Saving the Vines

*R*iding through the vineyards of Sonoma County

on a warm autumn day, Georges de Latour was aware of

the steady hoofbeats of his horse, the sway of the

wagon, the pungent but not unpleasant smell of moist

tartrate crystals in the wagon bed and the buzz of flies

— all normal and benign sensations. Yet he was keenly

aware of something else, an invisible yet monstrous

presence beneath the ground on both sides of the road.

With a frown he imagined that he could hear an insidious munching — the sound of vine roots being slowly but efficiently devoured by a nearly microscopic aphid called *phylloxera vastatrix.* De Latour had a terrible firsthand knowledge of this ravaging pest, for he remembered all too well the unnatural landscape of his family's withered vineyard in Daglan. He recalled as well the anguish of his parents and other vineyard owners as the vines of France, and then of all Europe, continued to die.

Phylloxera is indigenous to the Mississippi Valley, where it lives on native North American vines that are resistant to it. On especially resistant vines such as *Vitis rupestris,* the insect's population naturally stabilizes while it goes through a complex reproduction cycle; then its ecological role is that of a benign parasite something like a flea, annoying but not lethal. In fact, entomologists barely paid it any attention before it was introduced to France through experimental *rupestris* plantings in the 1850s.

On nonresistant vines phylloxera becomes a predator, multiplying ferociously as it devours roots and destroys the plant's ability to take in water and nutrients vital to photosynthesis. The first bugs to arrive in France must have thought they'd arrived in heaven — what a feast was there! Every vine was susceptible and there were no natural predators; they moved through the greater European vineyard with impunity.

In the process, the voracious root-sucker transformed the nature of wine forever. Today there are only a relatively few acres of ungrafted vines in the world, and their days are numbered. That's partly because the pest continues to spread, evolving as it moves (the California phylloxera infestation of the late twentieth century was reportedly due to a previously unknown biotype). Research into resistant rootstocks led to new hybrids; it gradually became clear that each rootstock performs best in certain combinations of soil and climate, which dovetailed comfortably with the ongoing effort of viticulturists to design plantings for specific sites. It is now accepted that choice of rootstock casts a "minority vote" in determining the character of wine from a given location, so that even in places where resistant rootstock is not strictly necessary (Chile, for example), vines growing on their own roots are increasingly in the minority.

Phylloxera's immediate effects on the significant portion of the European economy that revolved around the vine were catastrophic. In particular, the destruction affected thousands of small landholders who relied on grapes for income. The de Latours were among them. Indeed, Georges could be said to have a personal grudge against phylloxera, which had deprived him of an expected life on his native land and thus precipitated his expatriation. Now he saw his old nemesis in his adopted country. The insects were undeniably in the neighborhood, their subterranean presence indicated by expanded pockets of dying vines everywhere he looked.

The first signs of phylloxera began to appear in the early 1870s — about the same time the pest's commercial impact was being felt in Bordeaux. By 1873 its presence in Sonoma County was confirmed. Yet few people realized the extent of the danger to the state's vineyards. There is some irony in the fact that even while the plague was creeping through the vineyards there was tremendous optimism in the California wine community, fueled by the assumption that the European wine industry was finished — destroyed by phylloxera.

When Georges de Latour began visiting the wine country a decade later the plague was well advanced, and collective alarm was changing into panic, even despair. Still, he was one of a very few people in California who fully appreciated how dire the situation would become. With characteristic shrewdness, he also saw a business opportunity. He understood something that the average grape grower didn't quite grasp, because it was simply unimaginable to anyone who hadn't witnessed it. The truth was staggering: every single vineyard in California would have to be replanted on resistant

PHYLLOXERA
DAMAGED VINES
NEAR RUTHERFORD
CALIFORNIA

47

rootstock. Georges de Latour decided to go into the business of providing that valuable live commodity.

DISCOVERING
PROSPERITY

Once again, the years spent on the road in the wine country would prove valuable. The network of contacts and business relationships built while buying argols from wineries would make it possible to jump start any wine-related business that de Latour cared to enter. He had earned the respect of growers and vintners even before he began making wine; he often tasted his clients' wines, and they paid attention to his observations on blending and aging, as well as his opinions of which vineyards were outstanding. While living in Healdsburg, Georges de Latour made several close friends among Sonoma County growers. One such contact was Leopold Justi, who had vineyards and a small winery in Glen Ellen. Eventually Justi became his agent in the vineyard country north and west of Napa Valley.

De Latour's decision to import resistant vines was right on target. The vine importation business was an immediate and enduring success, and an outstanding example of how he was able to do something for his fellow man and make money at the same time. The importance of this contribution to the survival of California viticulture was immense, dovetailing neatly with an immense benefit to the financial viability of the fledgling Beaulieu Vineyard.

The phylloxera-resistant roots were available with a wide choice of grafted grape varieties. In a letter to Justi dated August 12, 1906, de Latour offered French grafted vines of the following varieties: in white — Folle Blanche, Semillon, Clairette, Chasselas, Pinot Blanc, Sauvignons Vert and Muscadets, and St. Emilion; and in red — Cabernet, Merlot, Malbec, Aramon, Grenache, Carignan, Grands Noirs de la Calmette, Petite Syrah, Alicante Boushet, and Petit Bouchet. Later he also listed Zinfandel and Mataro. With typical thoroughness he established his own nursery near Paris where the vines were grown, grafted, and prepared for shipment. The vines were shipped from the French port of Le Havre to New York, where they were transferred to rail cars.

The correspondence with Justi is full of the details of a burgeoning

business. The transactions mention the names of prominent wine producers of the day, including Peretti of Simi Winery, Sonoma Valley grower Charles Bundschu (who served as manager of Inglenook for several years), and prominent Sonoma growers such as Rossner and Chauvet, names still associated with vineyards that are prized for their pre-Prohibition Zinfandel and Petite Sirah plantings. The correspondence also contains tantalizing glimpses of early twentieth century Napa Valley vintages. For example, approaching the harvest in late August, 1906, de Latour remarked to Justi that, "My vineyard is looking fine. Have no mildew at all." On September 26, 1907 he wrote, "We have been compelled to stop picking grapes as we had not sugar enough here and the crop is very large." De Latour was not yet making wine, however. He was obviously headed in that direction; the profits from selling his fruit to the California Wine Association were vital to his plan.

By the end of 1906 he was doing a thriving business with Justi as his agent in Sonoma County, selling grafted French vines on *rupestris* St. George and #3309 rootstock. Justi's letterhead read "Winemaker & Dealer and Importer of Resistant Vines." The grapes were not only for wine. In March, 1908 Justi received 1,000 table grape vines, mostly Chasselas and Muscat. They had been ordered by the Home for Feeble-Minded Children in Glen Ellen. Always beneficent in his shrewd way, Georges de Latour gave the Home a ten dollar break on the order.

Prosperity not only buoyed the young Beaulieu Vineyard, but helped Georges de Latour grow into the lifestyle to which he seemed pre-accustomed. By 1908 he was making his Sonoma rounds in an automobile. We don't know what model that first car was, although we can guess it was a Ford. In any case, it was faster than a carriage — although it did have its little problems, as he told Justi in a letter dated August 18: "I beg to apologize for not having called last time I was in Sonoma County, but had positively no time, as I was in an automobile and it broke down." No doubt he was genuinely chagrined; he hated unreliability in other people and would have been embarrassed to seem the least bit undependable himself. It also would have hurt to miss an opportunity to conduct lucrative business. To atone for the lapse, he offered, "If you have to see anybody I will take you around in the automobile and you can take the train back to Glen Ellen."

Reading through the correspondence of that period, one can almost see the young Frenchman rubbing his hands over the prospect of ever-greater profits. While he was certainly horrified by the damage inflicted throughout the community by the infestation, especially at the level of small family businesses like Beaulieu, he must have relished the knowledge that there was no cure for the pest besides rootstock replacement. Phylloxera continued to provide good business right up to Prohibition, when vineyards were abandoned for another, no less insidious reason. As he noted in another late 1908 letter to Justi: "I noticed on my way many places destroyed by phylloxera. Those people must want vines badly. Try to see them next week, as I must send in the orders to have the vines here by the first of February."

As the *St. Helena Star* noted in October, 1911, "When it comes to quality, California is greatly indebted to Mr. G. de Latour, of Rutherford, who for some years has imported hundreds of thousands of the choicest French grafted vines, which have been planted in all the important vineyards of the State."

The so-called noble varieties such as Cabernet Sauvignon were not the only vines in demand. In fact, the temperamental nature and generally low yield of such vines made them less popular, to all but the most serious producers, than heavy-bearing varieties that would produce good wine under a wider range of conditions. Thus, as late as 1915 Georges de Latour was still helping to finance Beaulieu Vineyard with a brisk business in Grand Noir de la Calmette and other varieties that have long since become obscure.

By the middle of the first decade of the twentieth century, the de Latours were juggling three businesses. They still processed and sold cream of tartar to Stauffer; they were importing and selling millions of phylloxera-resistant vines; and they were building a *négociant* business, buying wine in bulk and reselling it. The next step, long planned and anticipated, would be to start producing their own wine. But that presented a problem. Georges de Latour was known as the man who could do everything, but even with

Fernande's shrewd business acumen he was overextended as the manager of a burgeoning empire. They needed a steady and capable right-hand man to run the day-to-day winery and vineyard operations.

They began looking for a superintendent. It took a cataclysmic event to bring the right man from half a world away.

DIGGING OUT
OF THE RUINS

On April 18, 1906 an earthquake of shocking magnitude struck along the San Andreas fault. The impact zone in northern California was nearly 300 miles long; horizontal slippage of twenty feet was recorded along the fault near Pt. Reyes. The event is barely mentioned in the annals of Beaulieu, but other wineries recorded costly damages, mostly due to toppled tanks. It was estimated that two-thirds of the stored wine in Napa Valley was lost. Downtown Napa received relatively light damage, while Santa Rosa was virtually destroyed. San Francisco was heavily damaged by the quake and much of it was consumed by a subsequent fire that raged for three days and nights. The U.S. Army was called out to fight the fire, and the soldiers used dynamite to blast a firebreak ahead of the flames. The dynamite corridor became Van Ness Avenue, one of the City's main north-south thoroughfares to this day.

In Lausanne, Switzerland just before Christmas that year, a young Italian bricklayer named Joseph Ponti stopped by a newspaper kiosk on his way home from the construction site where he was working. He picked up an Italian newspaper, *Il Corriere di Milano,* and noticed an advertisement placed by the City of San Francisco. The call was going out for bricklayers, masons, and others skilled in construction trades to rebuild the City from the ashes up. The pay was outstanding — ten to twelve dollars a day.

Ponti was twenty-three years old and had just been discharged from the Italian army; he'd only been in Switzerland a few months. He had a good job, and he'd made some friends, including a charismatic young man named Benito Mussolini who would go on to have quite a dramatic life himself. But Ponti kept looking at the ad, thinking about the winter in Switzerland versus the near-Mediterranean climate of San Francisco. Times were lean in Italy, and a lot of Italians were emigrating. Among them was his uncle, Joseph

Balconi, who was working in a place called the Napa Valley, not far north of the quake-ravaged city by the bay.

"That's my place," Ponti said to himself. "I'm going to America." After spending Christmas with his parents and brothers in Italy, he embarked for the New World, arriving in San Francisco on January 25, 1907.

The day after he arrived he had a job digging ditches for water and gas lines to replace the ones broken by the earthquake. Much of the city was still in ruins. Naked chimneys poked up through piles of rubble that used to be buildings. Reigning over it all atop Nob Hill was the shattered Fairmont mansion, with workers swarming antlike around its gaping walls. Rain poured down day after day, and thousands of people were living awash in canvas tents. Ponti had the address of a friend from back home who had a small hotel on Filbert Street in North Beach. His friend said, "I don't have any rooms, but as a friend and neighbor I'll give you a place to sleep." Ponti's bed was in the hayloft of the barn, above the horses. It was warm and dry; he liked it.

By that time he was out of shape, and his hands were soft. Blisters made it hard to use a pick and shovel, so the foreman, a Sicilian who had only been in San Francisco a little while himself, said, "You look like an intelligent boy. I have a carload of pipe down at Third and Townsend. Take

five or six men and a truck, and bring that pipe up here." Just like that, Ponti was out of the trenches, a crew foreman. That would prove to be typical of his progress in America.

Ponti had already written to his uncle in St. Helena. Within a week of his arrival in San Francisco he received a letter inviting him up to St. Helena, where his uncle was working for the Schilling Vineyard Company on Spring Mountain. One Saturday night the young immigrant boarded a ferry in San Francisco, got off in Oakland, made his way to Crockett on the Carquinez Strait and took a ferry across to Vallejo, then boarded a Southern Pacific train up the Napa Valley to St. Helena, arriving around noon on Sunday, February 2, 1907. His uncle met him at the station and took him to lunch at the Colombo Hotel. While they were eating lunch a man came in who knew Balconi. He was another Italian, John Pisoli, and Balconi introduced him to Ponti as the foreman of Beaulieu Vineyard.

"My nephew's just in from Italy," Balconi told Pisoli. "He's looking for work."

"I'm looking for a few men to work in the vineyard," said Pisoli. "It's down in Rutherford, about four miles from here." That night Ponti stayed with his uncle, and the next day Joe Pisoli came up with a springboard wagon and took him to Beaulieu Vineyard, where he would spend the rest of his working life.

Ponti worked in the vineyard all day, pruning vines. At the end of the day, Pisoli introduced him to Georges de Latour. Typically, his first conversation with his new employer was an argument; it set the tone for their long and often stormy relationship.

The energetic Frenchman, nearly thirty years older than the young Italian, liked Ponti's looks immediately. He also liked the fact that he spoke French.

"You look like an intelligent boy," he said (apparently prospective employers all had the same impression of this outgoing *paisano*). "I'd like you to learn the wine business. Would you care to do that? If you're interested, then instead of working in the vineyard, tomorrow morning come up to the house and I'll put you to work in the winery."

"Fine," said young Ponti. "What's the pay?"

"Thirty dollars a month, and board," said de Latour.

"Doing what?"

"Running the winery."

Ponti could see that the "winery" was nothing more than barrel storage. Clearly, he would be setting up a winery first and *then* running it. Having borrowed money from his family in Italy for the trip to America, he had to buy clothes — and on top of that he was a young man who needed to buy a beer on Saturday night. "I'm not afraid to work," he told his new boss, "but just thirty dollars a month is not quite enough. I need at least thirty-five."

The Frenchman frowned. "Thirty-five? Well, if you work out I'll raise you."

"If you don't mind," said Ponti, "I need the raise right away. Otherwise, I don't mind working in the vineyard."

They went back and forth. Finally, with a kind of grim amusement, de Latour said, "All right, I'll pay you thirty-five. Come up to the house in the morning and start bottling wine." That was it. The next morning Joseph Ponti went to the stable near the white Victorian house where Georges and Fernande de Latour lived, and a very old Frenchman (who died soon thereafter) showed him how to move wine from barrels into bottles. Working one barrel at a time, he would fill several crates with bottles of wine and take the crates across the county road to the Rutherford train station for shipment.

De Latour was not producing this wine, but buying it from other producers barrel by barrel as cash flow allowed. His main source was a winery in Livermore Valley operated by the brothers Herman and Ernest Wente. He had met them on his tartrate-purchasing rounds, beginning a business relationship that would last for decades and benefit both parties substantially. Now, he was buying their wine in bulk, then turning around and selling it again.

The wine was white, and fairly sweet. The buyer was the Catholic Church.

BUILDING A
BONA FIDE WINERY

*T*wo years later, the de Latours leased another winery. They had given up their lease on the Thomann winery when they decided they could make money faster by selling their grapes to the California Wine Association. The CWA was an outgrowth of the Napa Valley Wine Association, a coalition of wine producers who were members of the Bank of St. Helena. They made wine at the huge Greystone Winery north of St. Helena (which is probably where the first de Latour crop was vinified) and at several other large bulk wineries located throughout northern California. The CWA was the largest grape purchaser of the day. As the de Latours' vineyards came into production, they generated capital for expansion. Now, things were going well; the Beaulieu Vineyard Corporation was profitable. It was time to try again to become wine producers rather than *négociants*.

They located another unused winery, a small stone building on the Silverado Trail owned by a Napa County sheriff named Henry Harris (who would paradoxically prove to be zealous enforcer of the law during Prohibition). The structure was outfitted with a crusher, a press, and several redwood tanks. There was also a caretaker, an elderly man named Henry Stice who was known as a good winemaker. The de Latours hired Stice for the first crush, and Georges said, "I'm going to send a young man named Joseph Ponti over to you. I want you to teach him everything you know about making wine."

JOSEPH PONTI, BV
SUPERINTENDENT
FROM 1907–1950

Since Beaulieu had committed its entire crop of grapes to the California Wine Association for twenty years — and borrowed fairly heavily against the contract to buy and plant more vineyards — the de Latours had to purchase grapes to make their first wines. The 1909 crush at the Harris winery yielded some 50,000 gallons of wine, both white and red. The wines were blends, but the varieties (the whites were predominantly Green Hungarian and Golden Chasselas, and the reds mostly Zinfandel and Petite Sirah) were fermented separately in 1,300-gallon redwood tanks.

By that time the battle with phylloxera was nearly won, thanks in no small part to the de Latours. In the Napa Valley alone, grape acreage had increased from a low of 2,000 acres to about 16,000. But a new threat to the the wine industry was already looming. In vineyards all over California there were large hand-painted signs saying, "Prohibition will destroy these vineyards." The Eighteenth Amendment would not be passed for another decade, but Prohibition was already in the air.

Small winery owners were spooked; each year more of them closed their doors. Always looking ahead, Georges de Latour took notice of small wineries that went out of business. He'd tell Ponti, "I just purchased several tanks from so-and-so. I want you to go down and pick them up." Large tanks would be dismantled, but smaller ones (1,000 gallons or so) would be hauled intact by teams of horses. Through shrewd tank purchases, de Latour brought the little winery's production capacity up to around 65,000 gallons. Apparently his intent from the beginning was to use the Harris winery temporarily, because he also purchased other winemaking equipment, including a press and crusher, to outfit the stable at Beaulieu for wine production. The *St. Helena Star* reported that the stable at Beaulieu was being extensively renovated, ceilings added and floors reinforced, in preparation for winemaking.

Georges de Latour chose a good winery for his first real crush. It seems to have been better than the typical small winery of the time — modest but well-equipped, and thought out by someone who knew what he was doing (probably Stice). And Ponti couldn't have had a better hands-on education in wine production from the ground up. With the harvest fast approaching, the first task was to clean the winery and get it up and running. That started with clearing the place of rattlesnakes (there's nothing a snake likes better on a hot Napa Valley afternoon than a dark stone building), and cleaning out rats' nests. Then the big wooden tanks had to be recommissioned. Because the winery had been unused for several vintages, the tanks were dried out. They had to be filled with water, which at first leaked through gaps between the shrunken staves, before the wood swelled enough to close the cracks. Only then were they ready for wine.

The setup was efficient. The crusher was located on the second floor, just under the roof. A belt-driven conveyor ran from the big double doors up to the crusher, and a chute, or series of chutes, ran from the crusher back down into the fermentation room. The chutes could be moved from tank to tank as each was filled with must.

The fermentors were open-topped, and Stice showed Ponti how to punch holes in the floating cap of grape skins and seeds so that the fermenting juice could bubble up; keeping the cap moist, he explained, was essential

to prevent the formation of acetobacter which would turn the wine to vinegar. It was good, solid, old-fashioned country winemaking.

When fermentation was finished the wine would be racked into 180-gallon puncheons and hauled up to the stable at Beaulieu. When de Latour complained that the wine removals were going too slowly, Ponti explained that racking by gravity was naturally a slow process. De Latour promptly invested in a cast-iron "guzzling pump" — high-tech for its day — which moved 1,500 gallons per hour. The big horse-drawn freight wagon held four puncheons at a time, and they made several trips each day. By the end of December, 1909, the stable was filled with what would be the first wine sold under the Beaulieu Vineyard trademark.

The next year they made wine again at the Harris place, and hauled it up to the stable at Beaulieu. By the end of December, 1910, there were about 100,000 gallons of wine in puncheons stored at Beaulieu.

During the first part of the following year all the winemaking equipment purchased by the de Latours to outfit the Harris winery was hauled up to BV, where it joined equipment already in place which had been acquired at good prices in the first flush of panic at the prospect of Prohibition. For five years, de Latour and Ponti made wine in the stable. But even with the additions, the building was too small. It was also susceptible to flooding when the stream through the property jumped its banks, which happened fairly often. The last straw came in the winter of 1914, one of the wettest on record.

During the height of flooding, eyewitnesses reported seeing barrels floating out the doors of wineries. While Beaulieu wasn't mentioned specifically, the estate did flood that year, so it can be assumed that barrels were floating inside the winery.

In 1916 the de Latours built a new winery. It was a large concrete building with plenty of room to produce wine. They also finished planting at BV#2: twenty acres of Cabernet Sauvignon, fifteen of Pinot Noir, twelve of Mondeuse, and also some Semillon, Sauvignon Verte, and Franken (Sylvaner). During the following summer, the old winery was torn down. One of the men on the demolition crew was Joseph Ponti's nephew, young Louis Tonella.

Ponti is often overlooked in accounts of Beaulieu's history. In fact, in his way he was as important to its success as André Tchelistcheff. There is no substitute for a good superintendent, especially one with Ponti's practical skills and inventiveness. With Ponti in charge, Beaulieu could have gone on running smoothly without Georges de Latour, the way a ship can sail on an established course with a good crew and helmsman. The captain decides where it's going, but it's people like Ponti who make it go.

CHAPTER FOUR

This Earth Is Mine

$\mathcal{I}$n the first decade of the twentieth century, Georges de Latour was involved in four substantial businesses: buying and selling argols, importing resistant vines, buying and selling sacramental and "medicinal" wine, and, finally, producing branded table wines. Each endeavor contributed importantly to the de Latour family's mounting success. But the key to the entire story, the pivot on which the Beaulieu story turns, was altar wine.

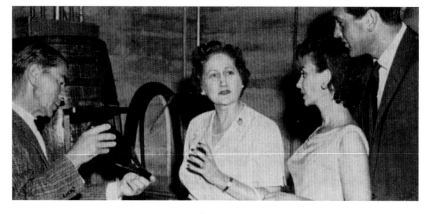

As the economic dark age of the "Noble Experiment" of Prohibition descends on the burgeoning American wine industry, one is tempted to imagine Georges de Latour experiencing a kind of epiphany — the realization that the practice of Roman Catholic Christianity requires wine. One might picture his revelation in the style of a Renaissance painting, with a choir singing Palestrina in the background. Kneeling in the little Rutherford church one lovely spring Sunday, Georges listens to the priest chanting a familiar litany, and suddenly the old lines have new meaning: "Who so eateth my flesh, and drinketh my blood, hath eternal life..."

The middle-aged Frenchman's eyes glitter. Christ himself ordered his disciples to sip a little wine once a week — could the government outlaw that? The de Latours' Sunday roast is washed down with a particularly good claret that afternoon, and on Monday morning Georges de Latour is contacting the Catholic Church Diocese of San Francisco.

This fantasy would have fit right into the melodramatic 1959 film *This Earth Is Mine* (filmed at various Napa Valley locations, including BV, Stags' Leap, and Beringer) in which Claude Rains rendered an over-the-top portrayal of a Napa Valley vintner ostensibly but inaccurately modeled on Georges de Latour. In all likelihood, however, the altar wine business did not result from a singular vision. Records are sketchy, but it appears that the saving grace of Beaulieu during Prohibition arose from the same combination of foresight and circumstance as the resistant rootstock business. De Latour must have seen the potential for altar wine while Prohibition was still just a gleam in Carrie Nation's eye, and when the franchise opened up he was simply prepared to take advantage of it. He obtained the warrant to produce altar wine for the Church well before the Eighteenth Amendment passed, and was thus positioned to become the first nationwide supplier of altar wine to Catholic churches across America. This brilliant stroke of foresight allowed Beaulieu's founder to aggressively expand his business while other wine producers were preparing to shut their doors or scramble to get by.

In fact, an unholy scandal may have pointed de Latour toward opportunity. In February of 1900 the *San Francisco Examiner* exposed shady dealings in St. Helena on the part of one Father Blake, head of the St. Helena Catholic Church. The *Examiner* alleged that Father Blake, who purchased sacramental wines from local producers for his own church, was taking kickbacks from wine producers in exchange for referring them to other parishes in need of altar wine. Father Blake's response appeared in a letter to the *St. Helena Star* on February 16, 1900. He denied everything, but paradoxically concluded by saying that he would henceforth refuse to assist other priests in procuring altar wines. Whether or not the allegations were true (nothing more was heard from either party in the controversy), that incident highlighted the existence of a ready market for sacramental wines — and the tantalizing fact that the Church itself had a distribution network already in place.

Thus, any wine producer who could secure that agency stood to move a lot of wine without the trouble and expense of actually having to market it. No warehouses, no outlets, no sales force, no advertising! That Georges de Latour saw this about the same time he bought the Thompson property is indicated by the fact that one of his first improvements on the ranch was to clean out the old stable to make room for barrels of wine, which he purchased from the Wente Winery in Livermore Valley.

By 1904 he had the endorsement of the Archdiocese of San Francisco. Thus, years before producing his own Beaulieu Vineyard wines, de Latour was supplying wine to the Catholic Church. In 1910 he established offices in New York as the Beaulieu Vineyard Distributing Company expressly for the altar wine trade. Five years later, amid the increasingly stormy debate leading up to the vote on the Eighteenth Amendment, advertisements for Beaulieu Vineyard altar wines appeared in print for the first time.

A NATION GOES DRY —
SORT OF

*T*he name of Andrew J. Volstead (R-Minnesota) will forever be associated with the bizarre episode in American history that President Calvin Coolidge called, "the greatest social experiment of modern times." Ironically, Volstead himself wasn't particularly anti-alcohol, just a good party man appointed to head the committee that drafted the legislation. The experiment involved

millions of bemused — and increasingly cranky — human guinea pigs as the dry years wore on. As sometimes happens in American politics, the general will of the people had been contravened by a vigorous minority, as described by Ernest Behr in his 1997 book, *Prohibition:*

Beyond the debate on the rights of reformers to regulate social behavior by force, restricting individual freedom in the name of better health, morality, and godliness, Prohibition was the rearguard action of a still dominant, overwhelmingly rural, white Anglo-Saxon Protestant establishment, aware that its privileges and natural right to rule were being increasingly threatened by the massive arrival of largely despised (and feared) beer-swilling, wine-drinking new American immigrants.

Among other lingering bad effects, Prohibition gave organized crime its institutional foothold in the American economy. Perhaps the only lasting positive outcome was that Susan B. Anthony and her colleagues were able to harness some of the widespread anger at domestic violence — blamed largely and for the most part rightly on male drunkenness — in strengthening their campaign to finally pass the Nineteenth Amendment (1927) granting women the right to vote.

Xenophobia took on righteous overtones in the Temperance marching anthem, the "Anti-Saloon War Song": "Tramp, tramp, tramp, the States are marching/One by one to victory/But we cannot win the fight/Until thirty-six are white/So we'll press the battle on from sea to sea." Possibly the racist connotation of "white" was unintended by most of the congregation, yet in retrospect it seems like a kind of collective Freudian slip expressing the true nature of the movement.

Not even the Bible was safe. In 1924 the Temperance Union hired Yale scholar Dr. Charles Foster Kent to censor it by toning down or changing references to wine. For example, two lines in Judges IX:13 were rewritten to read, "Shall I leave my juice that gladdens gods and men," and "He distributed to the whole assembled multitude a roll of bread, a portion of meat, and a cake of raisins."

Ironically, more than one wine producer made it through Prohibition selling pressed bricks of raisins to home winemakers. The cakes were labeled with a warning: "Caution — Will ferment and turn into wine," and salesgirls

in East Coast department stores carefully advised customers *not* to soak the bricks in water and place the liquid in a jug for twenty-one days because it would turn into wine, and *not* to bother stopping the bottle with a cork because that would only be necessary if fermentation occurred. The de Latours' St. Helena neighbors, Bertha Beringer and her brother, Charles, went into the raisin brick business whole-heartedly, and with very good results; they, too, were still in business at Repeal.

Everyone knows now — and knew at the time, for that matter — that Prohibition didn't come close to stopping the consumption of alcohol. As the folksy comedian Will Rogers slyly observed at the time, "Prohibition is better than no alcohol at all." However, it did make producing and selling alcoholic beverages of all kinds extremely problematic. Between 1920 and 1933, half a million people went to prison for violating the Volstead Act.

When it came to popular defiance of an unpopular law, the situation favored distillers over vintners. Not only did a smaller quantity of their product go farther than wine, barrel for barrel, it was easier to produce. A still could be set up practically anywhere, and the "mash" could consist of practically anything. Prunes, for example, remained a credible crop despite being well-known as a key distilling material. On the other hand, wine required acres of land and a high-profile cultivation and harvest regime. And unlike prunes, which were the most common material for illegal spirits in California, wine grapes had no other purpose than wine.

In Rutherford during the dry years, recalls longtime resident Louis Tonella (Joseph Ponti's nephew), it became fairly common to see large cars that rode strangely heavy and sluggishly on their wheels. At the Old Oaken Bucket saloon near the crossroads, Prohibition just made everyone a little more wary of strangers: "Sure, you could get a drink there, as long as they knew who you were. But if somebody was just passing through and went in there asking for a shot of something, they would probably be politely asked to leave." Meanwhile, the crop ratio in the valley began to favor prunes as vineyard owners threw in the towel.

In most of the wine country, especially Sonoma County, vineyards were part of diversified small farms. That allowed them to slip under the wire of the Eighteenth Amendment's allowance for home winemaking on a modest scale. The high concentration of small pre-Prohibition vineyards in Sonoma County which are still producing today (virtually all of them Zinfandel and Petite Sirah) is living proof that many growers made it through with little trouble.

It was a different story with commercial wine producers such as those concentrated in the Napa Valley. The overall effect of Prohibition on the valley's wine industry was nearly as devastating as phylloxera, from which it was just beginning to recover. But a few farsighted commercial vintners persevered — not so much through stubbornness as because they were simply unable to believe that something as sane and civilized as wine could possibly be banned forever.

Georges de Latour was foremost among them. With his diversified business and strict policy of reinvesting the profits in Beaulieu, he was clearly looking beyond Prohibition, and stood in a good position to take advantage of the calamity. When wineries began to close their doors in anticipation of Prohibition, Georges and Fernande de Latour bought up winery equipment at sale prices. When the full reality hit and vineyard land became available, they invested everything they could spare in land.

LOADING BARRELS
OF WINE ONTO A
RAILROAD CAR FOR
SHIPMENT AT THE BV
WINERY, C.1930

*T*hese real estate buys were all financed by wine. Georges de Latour's close ties with the Catholic Church (remember, several priests were on the original board of directors) gave him a largely exclusive franchise to produce altar wine for Catholic dioceses throughout the country. The only legal market for wine through those years proved to be a very thirsty market, indeed. Is it reasonable to suspect Catholic priests throughout the nation of bootlegging for their flocks? Perhaps not. Suffice it to point out that the volumes of wine moving through the diocesan network surpassed any ritual consumption by the most assiduous congregations if they were merely sipping symbolically at the communion rail.

A ready market for wine was not the only benefit of the de Latours' Catholic connection. Beaulieu was also able to acquire land from the Church, as well.

Since the Middle Ages, of course, the Church has been active in real estate (and in wine, for that matter), buying and selling land almost constantly as an integral part of its global corporate financial structure. For some time the Archdiocese of San Francisco had owned a large swath of land (thousands of acres at a time, in Joseph Ponti's recollection) in the heart of the valley around Rutherford. The St. Joseph's School and farm was purchased by the Catholic Church in May, 1904. The land had originally been owned by Napa Valley pioneer George C. Yount, who gave the property to his wife in 1864. When the Younts' granddaughter, Lillie, married Thomas Rutherford in October, 1880, the couple received 1,000 acres from Eliza Yount as a wedding gift. Sixteen years later the property was purchased in foreclosure by James W. Smith, who sold it to the Church for a token price.

Archbishop Riordan established St. Joseph's School for boys in 1904 with the Rev. Dennis O. Crowley as director. Each summer Crowley and his colleagues brought dozens of "angels with dirty faces" to Rutherford where they could benefit from the wholesome environment and clean living, doing character-building farm chores and picking prunes. There was a large house on the property, and a small church where Georges and Fernande de Latour often attended Mass on Sunday. Sometimes Mass was performed by the Archbishop himself. Father Crowley and Georges de Latour were good

THE PACKING AND
SHIPPING ROOM AT BV,
C.1930

friends and business associates from way back and may have had more in common than religion: reportedly both had been prospectors in the Sierra Gold Rush country. Thus, in countless small ways the family's bonds with the Catholic Church were strengthened.

The de Latours already owned 128 acres in Rutherford, purchased in 1903 and subsequently called BV#1. The Church made more of their property available as funds were needed, and the de Latours, being insiders, generally heard about the offers before they became public. In 1910 they purchased the 146-acre BV#2 from the Catholic Church. This vineyard was planted in stages and didn't come into full production until 1920. In 1923, de Latour bought the first blocks of BV#3 as tracts of 19.1 and 91 acres of the St. Joseph's School property.

Ponti, too, benefited from the de Latours' privileged position vis-à-vis the Church, acquiring some forty acres for himself just west of the Silverado Trail in 1923. (He later turned the property over to his nephew, Louis Tonella; Lou's son Ray now farms the property and continues to sell all of his Cabernet Sauvignon to BV.)

Apparently not all of this land buying was for grapes. According to Ponti, Georges de Latour had it in mind to subdivide some of the land. "Mr.

de Latour says he wanted me to be part of it, he says why didn't we buy that section down there, on the other side of the road (the Silverado Trail) and we'll divide it up and sell it in twenty-acre lots, something like that," Ponti said in 1973. They had a Napa surveyor draw a map, but Ponti, fearing debt, backed out of the deal. De Latour sold a thirty-acre plot along the Silverado Trail to a friend named Fitzpatrick who worked for the Donohoe-Kelly Banking Co. in San Francisco (one of the major lenders to Beaulieu in the beginning), but he kept the rest of the land to grow prunes and grapes. Ponti planted a vineyard for Fitzpatrick and managed it with Beaulieu crews, sending Fitzpatrick monthly bills. Apparently the accounts payable took some of the romance out of the wine country lifestyle. Not long after that Fitzpatrick tired of the venture and sold the land back to Beaulieu at a buyer's price — which may have been what was intended all along.

Meanwhile, the altar wine business was thriving. Georges de Latour (and through him, suppliers such as the Wente and Martini families) were shipping communion wines to churches throughout the country. The Wente family, whose vineyards were in Livermore (east of San Francisco), sold about 30,000 gallons of sweet Semillon (which they called Sauterne) to BV each year. It was the only wine they made, and it all went to Georges de Latour.

The altar wine market was a microcosm of the larger wine market in in one respect particularly: there were regional tastes, and even diocesan tastes. Churches in New Orleans, where the priests were mostly French, wanted red wine on the dry side. Churches in Minnesota wanted sweet white wine. In California, they favored the fortified wine called Angelica — except in cosmopolitan San Francisco, where the Marist fathers poured dry red wine at the Communion rail. Many priests purchased young wine in barrels, and aged it in their own cellars as the European clergy has done since medieval times.

As the demand for sacramental wines increased, the production capacities of the old stable and winery on the Beaulieu estate, already expanded in several directions over the years, were no longer adequate. The de Latours faced a choice: build a brand-new winery, or buy a serviceable existing one.

For some time de Latour had been eyeing a large stone winery just across the county road from Beaulieu. Somehow it just seemed as though it should belong to Beaulieu. The Ewer-Atkinson Winery had been designed by

Hamden McIntyre (an early manager of Inglenook) in Senator Seneca Ewer's heyday but had since declined. It was now being offered for sale by Senator Ewer's son, Fred. In the spring of 1923 Georges de Latour purchased the Ewer Winery and expanded Beaulieu's production dramatically.

Virtually every drop of the 1923 vintage disappeared to slake the apparently inexhaustible thirst of Catholic parishes throughout the country. During the next spring and summer, construction crews worked feverishly to add another wing to the winery.

On February 15, 1924, the Archbishop of San Francisco sent a letter to Beaulieu Vineyard. He was writing, he said, to "express my unqualified approval of the very superior quality and high standard of the wines which you furnish each year." He went on, "In my opinion Mr. Georges de Latour, the President of your Company, is one of the best winemakers in California, and I can vouch for the absolute purity and good quality of the Mass wine which is made at your extensive vineyards; and, as a further evidence of my confidence in his winemaking ability, the grapes grown in the vineyards of St. Joseph's Agricultural Institute at Rutherford, California, are disposed of to you for the production of Mass wine."

This may well have been a spontaneous note dashed off in a momentary paroxysm of admiration — but three-quarters of a century after the fact it reads suspiciously like propaganda. For whose eyes was it meant? As the Archbishop goes on, we can almost hear the words being read in a court of law: "The fact that your wine is made under the direct supervision of Reverend D.O. Crowley, who has acted in that capacity for the last twenty years, is in itself an assurance of the high standard of your product. Therefore it is a pleasure for me to know that the Beaulieu Vineyard is supplying such a very large number of the Clergy with wine for the Holy Sacrifice, and that the demand for your wine is ever increasing. This fact is fully sustained by the records in this office." In any case, the Archbishop's vote of confidence served to expand the Beaulieu grape supply still further.

In 1926, at the heart of Prohibition, the Alcohol Tax Unit of the U.S. Treasury Department stopped issuing permits for the transfer of wine from one bonded winery to another, unless it was used for blending. Buying finished wine from another winery was disallowed, a measure that had a direct impact on (and may have been aimed at) Beaulieu Vineyard. That meant Georges de Latour was unable to buy wine from the Wentes unless he blended it, which was impractical because the sweet Sauterne would initiate fermentation in any other wine into which it was introduced.

The crisis called for ingenuity on Georges's part. He quickly came up with a plan. The Wente Winery was bonded, so the Wentes could make wine; but they couldn't sell it commercially. They only made one wine, the sweet Sauterne, expressly as altar wine, for sale to BV. Georges said to the Wentes, "You're not doing anything with your bond. Why don't you transfer it over to Beaulieu Vineyard? Then we can carry on and we will give it back to you after Repeal, if and when it comes."

The Wentes agreed, and the Wente Winery became Beaulieu Vineyard's Bonded Winery Number Two. That allowed the Wentes to put barrels of their wine on railroad cars at BV's direction and ship directly to the BV distributors in New York, Chicago, and other parts of the country. Once again, Georges de Latour had demonstrated that there is almost always a way around any problem, if you look hard enough for it.

CABERNET VINES IN BV#2, LOOKING NORTHWEST TO MT. ST. JOHN, WITH INGLENOOK WINERY IN THE MIDDLE BACKGROUND, 1930S

ESTABLISHING A LEGACY

While the Ewer Winery was undergoing expansion in 1924, Georges and Fernande's twenty-year-old daughter Hélène married a French aristocrat, the

Marquis Galcerand de Pins. The wedding took place in St. Mary's Cathedral with the new Archbishop, Fr. William Hanna, doing the honors. It was a fabulous social event; it was said that the glow remained for years.

Hélène and Galcerand had a daughter in 1925. Dagmar de Pins was named after her paternal grandmother, who had been named after the Danish Princess Dagmar, the wife of Czar Alexander III of Russia. Dagmar grew up in San Francisco, Rutherford, and France, as her mother had. Her early bout with polio kept her somewhat isolated until her full recovery at fifteen, but in time she attended the same school as her mother, Sacred Heart Convent.

In 1925 the de Latours expanded their company again by purchasing the French-American Winery in Rutherford — but not for wine production. The building had been previously damaged by fire, and rather than rebuilding it as a winery, the de Latours erected a large prune dehydrator. They were, in fact, prune farmers on nearly as large a scale as they were grape growers. Much of the land they had purchased from St. Joseph's School had prune orchards on it, and the expense of converting the prunes to vineyard was too great to undertake all at once. Also, there was quite a demand for prunes at that time, and during several subsequent periods; the prune story runs parallel to the story of wine through much of Napa Valley history. Thus the lucrative prune paid for much of Beaulieu's physical expansion through the Prohibition years.

The third block of BV#3, for example, was used for prunes. This new chunk of St. Joseph's School was purchased in 1928. It embraced some fifty-nine acres; its legal owner was Hélène de Latour. The fruit was prepared for market in the prune dehydrator now located on the site of the French-American Winery. That prune dehydrator operated until the late 1930s, and Rutherford old-timers still recall the pervasive, sometimes oppressive odor of prunes being dried over gas burners that were fired up day and night.

One day Joseph Ponti was invited to lunch at Beaulieu with Georges, Fernande, and Hélène. At one point there was a lull in the conversation. Georges had been uncharacteristically silent for several minutes. Rather abruptly he said, "Hélène, I want you to promise me that if you ever want to sell out after I die, you won't sell Beaulieu."

FROM LEFT, HÉLÈNE, DAGMAR, FERNANDE, GALCERAND, AND RICHARD (FERNANDE AND GEORGE'S SON)

Hélène promised, and the meal went on. But neither the Beaulieu superintendent nor the Marquise de Pins ever forgot that moment.

On the eve of Repeal in 1933, Georges and Fernande purchased the last piece of BV#3 (32.6 acres). At that time W.L. St. Amant became vice president and general manager of BV for a short period.

Prohibition ended when Congress passed the Twenty-First Amendment, which repealed the Eighteenth Amendment and made it legal once again not only to drink alcoholic beverages, but to produce them. Legally, it was as if Prohibition had never happened, except for the fact that only one winery came out of the dry years with its production, marketing, and distribution intact: Beaulieu Vineyard. In December 1933 the *San Francisco Chronicle* reported that the BV winery contained some 1,200,000 gallons of wine. In 1933 alone, altar wine sales totalled more than 200,000 gallons.

A measure of BV's success through the end of Prohibition can be gleaned from a few key numbers: On January 1, 1924 the books showed an uninvested budget surplus of $107,000. At that meeting the directors decided to issue the company's first dividend — $25 per share on a total of 4,000 shares. In 1925 the surplus was only about $55,000. That occasioned some heated discussion of whether the dividend was a good idea. The dividend was maintained, but lowered to $10 per share.

In 1928 the surplus was up again, to over $131,000, and the following year it reached $245,000. In that year Georges de Latour was paid $24,000 as president of the company, Fernande de Latour was paid $9,000 as vice president and secretary, and their daughter Hélène received $7,500 as secretary.

By contrast, in 1929 a worker at Beaulieu Vineyard was paid twenty-five to forty cents an hour. A man working on the bottling line would get a check at the end of two weeks for about $25. "Money went a long way in those days, but you didn't accumulate or have a lot of cash on hand," recalls Joseph Ponti's nephew, Louis Tonella. Lou had gone to work on the bottling line in 1929 at the age of seventeen. He lived with his uncle and aunt, Mr. and Mrs. Ponti, on Niebaum Lane, and eventually built a house there (for about $3,600!).

Lou noticed early on that most of the workers in the Rutherford neighborhood spent their money at the general store next to the Beaulieu Vineyard winery. While working for the de Latours, he kept watching all that money being spent at the store in Rutherford. He finally left BV in 1935 and bought the store with Julius Caiocca, who later became a county supervisor and was one of the founders of the Napa Valley Green Belt, or Agricultural Preserve. The partners paid about $7,000 for the store. Joseph Ponti loaned his nephew the money for his share.

"We sold everything," recalled Lou more than sixty years later. "Jeans,

boots, vineyard rope, sulfur, hats, general merchandise, anything and everything. We had a butcher shop, a barber shop, a post office."

He was in a position to sell everything because the people who worked for Beaulieu Vineyard, unlike the depleted work forces at other vineyards and wineries, had money to spend. Their employers, Georges and Fernande de Latour, had not only made it through Prohibition — they had prospered. And that put them in a position to prosper even more. As Ernest Wente pointed out, "When Prohibition ended, BV was in the driver's seat."

BV GRAPE PICKER, 1940S

opposite:
LOADING BARRELS OF WINE FOR SHIPMENT BY RAIL TO THE EAST COAST, C.1934

CHAPTER FIVE

The Maestro

*I*n the years immediately following Repeal,
California wineries sent a great deal of wine back East.
Unfortunately, much of it was beneath the basic
standard of quality even for a newly legal market for
alcoholic beverages. In the rush to meet the almost
unbelievable demand, there were inevitable compromises
on the production end. Shipping wine in tanks and
barrels made it subject to tampering by distributors, who
were sorely tempted to water it down to stretch profits.

It's often been said that the greatest impetus to home winemaking in America was the quality of American commercial wine in the 30s. By all accounts, BV's wines were superior to most, yet corners were surely cut in a production facility strained by the surge in volume.

Georges de Latour was painfully aware of the situation. He had to stand among his employees as barrels of rejected wine were rolled out of train cars on the winery's loading dock. The moral discomfort of having one's product returned was deepened considerably by a sinking bottom line. The de Latour style of aggressive expansion meant that virtually all expected profits were earmarked for projected expenditures, or monies borrowed against them. That many of those expenses were related to the de Latours' lifestyle in Rutherford, San Francisco, and Europe signaled a bad habit that would punish them more than once.

But anybody could see that it ended up costing more to make bad wine than it would to make good wine. De Latour once again showed his keen competitive instinct in a concise series of remedial steps.

The first was to borrow a page from Bordeaux history and move toward bottling all of his wine at the winery rather than shipping most of it in bulk. That would allow him to control the quality — at least, if the wine that reached consumers was bad, it could be blamed on the producer rather than on mistreated barrels, bad storage, or offsite bottling practices. It would also prevent unscrupulous dealers from stretching BV wines with inferior wines or even water, which was a common practice among wholesaling businesses that had been formed in the freewheeling atmosphere of Prohibition. In one case, a shipment of wine from Rutherford arrived in Milwaukee as little more than grapey water.

The de Latours then sued their Los Angeles distributor for adulterating BV wine. It was probably the first litigation in the U.S. addressing that issue. The court decided in BV's favor, but that was like slamming the door after the horse was out of the barn. In the end, the only practical way to control the quality of wine reaching the marketplace would be to bottle all of it at the winery, a goal that wasn't fully realized until the late 1950s.

The next step was to revitalize the management team. Unfortunately, that meant removing manager Charles W. Fay, now in his seventies and unable to keep up with developments in the fast-changing marketplace. Fay, a

former San Francisco postmaster during the Wilson administration and secretary to Senator Phelan, was a big wheel in the California Democratic Party. He was also on the Bank of America's board of directors. He had been appointed manager in 1934, but by 1936 it was apparent that the challenges of the time called for someone younger and in better health. Replacing him wouldn't be easy. Fay's connections had been valuable to the company, and he had become a personal friend of the de Latour family. Still, business was business, so late in 1936 (on Christmas Day, according to company legend) Georges asked Charlie Fay to step down. Fay took it harder than expected; within months he suffered a fatal stroke.

De Latour also hired an experienced public relations man named Leon Munier to define and promote BV's image. Inspired by Champagne's success with roving ambassadors who made sure the beautiful people always had bubbly on hand, Georges also hired the charismatic Jack Stanton. It was Stanton's job to travel the country, personally introducing key people to Beaulieu wines.

One of Fay's last acts as manager was to hire a twenty-five-year-old bookkeeper named Otto Gramlow. At the time Gramlow was working for the Bank of America. He had started as a messenger and worked his way up, attending night school (with assistance from his employer) to learn accounting.

When he first started working for the bank in the 1920s, he recalled later, it was in the branch at the corner of Market and Montgomery. The Marquise de Pins did her banking there; she was known among the clerks as the Countess. When this glamorous woman came into the bank, Otto Gramlow and his coworkers would peer out of their offices. "The fellows would say, 'Hey, come on in, the Countess is here.' Well, everybody had to go out to look at the Countess. Of course, she was a very attractive young woman."

Georges de Latour and Bank of America founder A.P. Gianini were good friends, and for several years the two firms had their offices next door. In 1936 one of Gramlow's colleagues in the Bank of America accounting department was offered a job at Beaulieu. He didn't accept it, but recommended Gramlow, who did. When Gramlow told friends he had been hired by Beaulieu Vineyard, they said, "Oh, you're going to work for de Latour." Even in the late 30s, the name of the estate's founder was better known than the brand.

If Gramlow showed up for his new job blithely, he soon found that the job wouldn't be easy. "When I came to work for the company, I found the books in very poor shape," he later recalled. "Acquisition of capital assets was very poorly recorded. In fact, I worked with the CPAs for several months trying to reconstruct the books to find out what he paid for each piece or parcel of land, and it was apparently impossible." He soon caught on that he wasn't meant to know too much. Georges de Latour, the consummate money-juggler, was always circumspect in business matters, a habit developed while keeping several businesses feeding one another during precarious financial times.

THE DREAM OF
WORLD-CLASS WINE

*M*eanwhile, even Mother Nature had participated in making 1936 one of the most momentous years in Beaulieu history. Added to the dynamics of reinventing a business was a spectacular vintage.

Napa Valley vineyards suffered severe frost damage in the spring of 1936. It was the worst frost season on record, striking late when the vines were already well into the first surge of growth, withering the tender young shoots

and severely limiting the subsequent crop. There was also considerable damage among the approximately 800 acres (the most since Prohibition) of newly planted and grafted vines in the valley, several hundred of which belonged to BV.

After that ugly beginning, the rest of the season was fine. Georges de Latour knew that superb vintages often result from hard winters and cold springs, which are common in Bordeaux yet relatively rare in California. He exulted as he walked among his vines in the days leading up to harvest. The Cabernet Sauvignon looked magnificent. There were just a few bunches on each vine, but they were beautiful bunches of uniformly small, dark purple grapes that exploded with tangy flavor when he popped them in his mouth. He chewed the skins lightly, pleased with their softness and the complete absence of any green or unripe character.

"These grapes will make a great wine," he told Ponti. As usual, they kept the Cabernet Sauvignon from BV#1 and #2 separate throughout fermentation, and put the new wine into the best barrels. De Latour tasted from those barrels frequently and with mounting excitement as the wine coalesced after malolactic fermentation and began to show its power and depth.

Charles W. Fay's replacement was Lorenzo M. "Nino" Fabbrini, the

suave, Italian-born assistant manager of San Francisco's grand Palace Hotel. Nino's first job was to open national distribution channels for estate-bottled wine. Most of the wine BV produced was still being sold in bulk, except on the West Coast where about 3,000 cases were bottled. Fabbrini's genteel Old World marketing style would eventually prove too polite and reserved for the increasingly competitive wine market. However, he was effective in placing Beaulieu wines in first-rank restaurants and hotels. And he executed one masterstroke that effectively jumped all the competition, when he went to New York and contracted with Park & Tilford to distribute Beaulieu wines labeled with the words "bottled at the winery."

Of course, the most important step in consolidating BV's preeminence was to make sure that the quality of the wine that went into those bottles justified all that expense. George de Latour needed a winemaker. No, he needed an enologist — the practitioners of what passed for winemaking at that time in California didn't have high enough standards. They were oriented toward making wine that was good enough for the domestic market, but de Latour had the global market in mind. His early awareness of the Bordelais wine world made him predisposed toward export, and he intended to meet international standards. Since those standards were set by the French wine industry, he determined to hire a French enologist, someone who knew the meaning of fine wine and knew how to produce it.

De Latour himself certainly knew the meaning of fine wine. Here his early upbringing came into play. It's not known whether his family's vineyard was oriented toward the highest quality, but even the most basic *crus bourgeois* grower was aware of how high the standard was set; they all had the well-known châteaux to look up to, if only to show what was possible.

Those standards were on everybody's mind in the late nineteenth century — not just wine producers, but a new generation of sophisticated consumers enjoying a supercharged world economy. That critical way of looking at wine would lead to the classification system of 1855 by which the significant Bordeaux properties are still ranked today. Although seen from the beginning as a means of organizing and enhancing the Bordeaux wine market, the classification gained lasting credibility from the fact that it purported to formalize long-term consensus. Its formal basis was a consideration of the prices consistently paid for various wines during the previous 100 years. Georges de Latour was certainly aware of all of the issues involved in the classification, and no doubt had his own opinions.

Certainly, he knew the difference between a château-bottled Claret and the kind of wine families purchased by the gallon to wash down their meals (or bought by the clergy to serve at the communion rail), and he meant to produce the highest quality in both categories. After years of interacting with the northern California wine community and living in the wine country, he was intimately familiar with the range of quality not just of wines, but of the vineyards that produced them. Furthermore, he knew that the collection of vineyards he had assembled in the Napa Valley represented some of the best vineyard land anywhere, capable of producing wines that would stand with the best in the world.

Georges de Latour was not the first person to realize that California could produce world-class wines. There had been several vintners (not incidentally, many of them French) working toward that goal in the nineteenth century, before phylloxera and Prohibition. But Georges de Latour was the first twentieth-century California vintner to make real the dream of world-class wine produced in California.

He was always thinking ahead. The continuing prosperity of the de

Latour family was foremost in his mind, but so was continued improvement of the quality of BV wines. The decision to begin bottling at the winery after Prohibition was a big step in that direction, as was the hiring of a UC Davis enologist, Professor Leon Bonnet, to oversee winemaking (much to the displeasure of superintendent Joseph Ponti, who was the real hands-on winemaker and who took a great deal of pride in his wines). But he still needed the one element that could bring it all together. To produce world-class wines, he needed a world-class winemaker — and at that time, the caliber of winemaker he needed could only be found in France.

THE STORY OF ANDRÉ TCHELISTCHEFF

While Georges and Fernande de Latour were struggling to build their California business in the years leading up to Prohibition, Europe burst into flames. The momentous events taking place on the other side of the world would prove to have a direct impact on Beaulieu Vineyard.

It would have been hard to imagine thundering artillery and the roar of pitched battle in the serene stillness of a Napa Valley afternoon, where you could hear a bee approaching long before you saw it. Yet terrible battles were being fought and tremendous changes were underway. The chaos would give birth to a new Europe. It would also disperse some remarkable Europeans throughout the world. A dark, intense Russian named André Tchelistcheff would wind up at Beaulieu Vineyard and become one of the most influential men in the history of California wine.

Had Georges de Latour ever heard of André Tchelistcheff? Probably not. De Latour and his son-in-law the Marquis de Pins only met with André for a few minutes at the Institut National Agronomique in Paris, and must have hired him on the strength of a recommendation by Institut faculty head Professor Marsais. A renowned enologist himself, Marsais may actually have been the first choice; in any case, he spoke highly of the young man he introduced to de Latour and the Marquis that morning. That the small, dark, and handsome Russian enology graduate would become one of the great winemakers of his time couldn't have been suspected by any of them, even one with an insight as penetrating as Georges de Latour's.

André's impact on the California wine industry was immense. He effected a major boost in basic quality simply by his insistence on sanitation. As a second-generation devotee of the nineteenth-century microbiology pioneer Louis Pasteur, he understood the presence of an invisible world of microbes that had to be managed just as much as the vineyards. His introduction of temperature-controlled fermentation helped make white wine a viable commercial product in California for the first time. And because white wines could be delivered to the marketplace earlier after the vintage than reds, the flow of cash to wineries and growers increased dramatically, enabling further widespread improvements in vineyards and wineries. André's insistence on converting the BV vineyards to European methods of cultivation and pruning had an immediate and obvious effect on wine quality. He also pioneered the use of the laboratory as a multifaceted winemaking tool (another influence transmitted from the Pasteur circle in France). His rigorous approach to enology was felt throughout the California wine world well into the 1980s.

All of that was embodied in Beaulieu Vineyard wines from 1938 onward — and one bottling in particular. The 1936 Georges de Latour Private Reserve, released in 1941, was the first California wine to be accepted throughout the world as a *premier cru*-level bottling. It was also the state's first intentionally varietal Cabernet Sauvignon to gain international recognition, and its success set the Napa Valley on a steady course toward specialization in Bordeaux-type cuvées. Georges de Latour Private Reserve remains a benchmark of style and quality in California wine.

It's easy to say that André Tchelistcheff's work was the fulcrum on which the Napa Valley was lifted into the first rank of the world's wine regions. But there's much more to it than that. It wasn't so much what he did — most of it would have happened sooner or later in the natural course of evolution — but rather how he did it. He was certainly a gifted winemaker, a

GEORGES DE LATOUR,
CENTER, AND VISITORS,
INSPECTING BV#2
WITH THE RANCH
FOREMAN (POINTING),
1939

brilliant enologist, and an insightful viticulturist. More than that, André Tchelistcheff was a leader and a teacher, who led and taught by example.

He loved working with young people, who almost invariably considered him a mentor or even a father. Until the very end of his long life he retained a youthful enthusiasm and vigor, which he attributed to the loss of his own youth in the cauldron of revolution and war.

Ironically, much more is known about the life of Georges de Latour's star enologist than about the Beaulieu Vineyard founder himself.

André Victorovich Tchelistcheff was born in Moscow on December 7, 1901 (November 24 in the old Russian calendar). His family traced its aristocratic roots to the thirteenth century. According to the family's own legend, their ancestor was knighted by the great Russian hero Prince Alexander

Nevsky after showing particular bravery in the pivotal Battle of the Ice against barbarian invaders. The family's several branches produced a number of illustrious figures, including doctors, jurists, and the neo-Romantic painter Pavel Tchelitchew (1898–1957), André's cousin.

The Tchelistcheffs were an established old-money family by the time André was born. On their estate in the forested Kaluga province, outside Moscow, they bred Borzoi hounds and Orloff horses. The Tchelistcheff line of Borzois was famous. In a frame on the wall of André's Napa Valley house is a leather and horsehair whip that belonged to André's grandfather. It was one of his most cherished possessions. The whip had been used to help control the dogs on a hunt — or, sometimes, to save them. When André was young he once saw his grandfather wrap the whip around the neck of a wolf that had turned on a dog, pulling the wolf away in time to save the dog for another hunt.

André had two brothers, Victor and Nicolai, and three sisters, Olga, Anne, and Alexandra. His father, Victor Tchelistcheff, was a scholar of Russian legal reform and the chief justice of the Russian Imperial Court of Appeals in Moscow, under the jurisdiction of the popular Social Democrat politician Alexander Kerenski.

The drawn-out melodrama known as the Russian Revolution arose from a complex web of social, economic, political, and philosophical

conflicts, but at its core it was a class struggle. As Russia became destabilized by the unforeseen ferocity of World War I, several revolutionary parties vied for control. Czar Nicholas Alexander was toppled in February, 1917. Less than a year later, Kerenski's provisional government was deposed by the Bolsheviks; as the conflict became more brutal, Russia collapsed into civil war. The war would last four years, and its repercussions would dramatically affect global history.

Victor Tchelistcheff was a liberal intellectual, and a proponent of the February Revolution. Twelve months later, when the Bolsheviks gained power, Victor was forced into hiding. According to André, he never spent a single night with his family in Russia after the October Revolution.

The Bolsheviks destroyed the Tchelistcheff estate in Kaluga province — strangling the Borzoi hounds and confiscating the Orloff horses, then burning the house with its library of rare books in five languages. The family moved to an uncle's estate nearby. Kerenski was able to warn Victor Tchelistcheff about the coming trouble; Victor called in a favor from a man he'd helped during the 1905 troubles, who helped the family obtain false passports. When the time came to leave, they literally walked away on their real passports, which were hidden in their shoes.

When André told the story in later years, he often cited one detail in particular to characterize the trauma: they were given twenty-four hours notice to leave the uncle's estate (which had been confiscated by the revolutionary government) and forced to leave with nothing but two changes of clothes.

LEFT TO RIGHT:
ANDRÉ TCHELISTCHEFF,
ALDO FABBRINI,
GEORGE WINKLER,
OTTO GRAMLOW, A.J.
SANCHIRICO AND
A.J. GANDER,
RUTHERFORD, 1956

opposite:

A HAND DATED BOTTLE
OF 1936 GEORGE DE
LATOUR PRIVATE
RESERVE CABERNET
SAUVIGNON

Everything else was left behind when the Tchelistcheff family became refugees.

Victor decided to take his family south to the Ukraine, where he would join the White Army for the coming civil war. By that time, however, the Ukraine was occupied by German forces. The way to Kiev was blocked. After spending several nights in a town near the cordon, they paid a local man a large sum of money to guide them through. But once they got close they were on their own — then they switched back to the official identity documents they'd concealed in their shoes. Since part of the family came from Prussia, they all spoke German, and were able to talk their way through the checkpoints by passing as Germans. Finally, they arrived in Kiev, where Victor became the White Russian Secretary of Justice.

As the start of Prohibition in the United States was forcing Georges de Latour to shift his resources into the altar wine business, young André Tchelistcheff entered the Military Academy in Kiev, and subsequently joined the southern White Army as a lieutenant in the Krasnodar Infantry. He was in the army from 1919 until the end of the Russian Civil War in 1922. After the White Army's surrender, his unit was made to work for several months in the Crimean coal mines before being conscripted to suppress the Bulgarian Revolution.

During a battle in the Crimean Peninsula, André and his troops came under heavy machine-gun fire during a snowstorm. André was presumed killed. The family was actually notified of his death, and a memorial service was performed. In fact, he was only missing in action — he'd become disoriented in the blizzard and crawled into a thicket for shelter. Found unconscious by a detail of Cossacks picking up their dead, André was thrown across a horse for transport. Later he woke up in a field hospital with both legs frozen. After three weeks of soaking in olive oil, the tissue thawed with no lasting damage.

André was a great walker all his life. Even a year before his death he'd go out among the vines with BV winemaker Joel Aiken and the rest of the new generation winemaking staff, returning home in the evening to tell his wife proudly, "I out-walked the kids in the vineyard today."

He never forgot the suffering his family endured during their flight from Moscow, or his own traumatic experiences during the civil war, such as shivering on the top of a train car rolling through miles of blood-reddened snow and frozen corpses. In many ways the story is accurately reflected by the film epic, *Dr. Zhivago*. It was André's favorite movie. His widow, Dorothy, recalls that he watched it twenty times or more, and each time he saw it, he cried.

André's formal education began at the Institute of Agricultural Technology in Brno, Czechoslovakia. He was drawn to the natural sciences; his dream throughout life was to own a farm. He loved raising animals, and during the 1930s published two books on poultry raising in France. His scientific education was vast — at various times he studied animal physiology, zoology, agricultural science and engineering, chemistry, and physics — and he considered that knowledge the basis of his successful career in enology.

That career began in 1929, at a research laboratory in Dubrovnik. Two years later he moved briefly to Belgrade, where his father was living, and then he and his new wife (the daughter of a Russian expatriate living in Belgrade) moved to France. At first he had a poultry farm in Bouilley les Trous. But tragedy struck during the second year of operation, in the form of a cataclysmic hailstorm with egg-sized chunks of ice that killed all the animals and destroyed the crops.

It was only after the failure of his farm that André decided to study viticulture and enology. A revolution had sent him to France; now, a hailstorm moved him a step closer to California.

André encountered California wines for the first time at the 1937 Paris Exposition, where he tasted a Wente Sauterne, Valle de Oro (the same wine, more or less, that the Wentes had sold to BV as altar wine during Prohibition; the Wentes began bottling their own wine in 1934, just after Repeal), and an Inglenook Traminer. The Traminer didn't move him at all, he said later, because it was made from the inferior "pink" Traminer and not the Alsatian Gewürztraminer. However, the Wente wine gave him a very good impression of California's potential.

At that time he was working and studying at both the Pasteur Institute and the Institut National Agronomique in Paris, where he worked as an assistant to Professor Paul Marsais conducting research in fermentation science, a subject which at that time, he said later, was "absolutely foreign to California — I would say scientifically, phonetically, or philosophically."

One morning André was summoned to his professor's office to meet two well-dressed, high-mannered men. Georges de Latour and his son-in-law, the Marquis de Pins, were looking for a specialist in enology and viticulture to manage wine production at the de Latour estate in California. André had already been offered similar jobs in France, Chile (where one of his colleagues had become a professor of enology), and the Chi Foo region of Manchuria, China, but as he put it later, "there was great pressure at that time toward America," particularly from his wife's family.

Getting the new BV enologist to California was no simple matter. At a dinner at the U.S. embassy in Paris, de Latour sat next to President Roosevelt's Secretary of Agriculture. Bringing all his considerable charm to bear, he informed her that he was a Napa Valley wine producer and that he was in the process of importing an enologist from France. To his utter shock, she told him it would be impossible. America was still in an economic depression, she pointed out, and unemployment was high. She added that wine was a luxury industry and therefore not a high priority.

Nonetheless, the next morning de Latour took André to the embassy. He had just launched into an impassioned statement of their case when the vice-consul interrupted. "I'm sorry, Mr. de Latour," he said, "but this is impossible."

In desperation, de Latour sent a wire to his staff in San Francisco, ordering them to contact the newly formed Wine Institute. The founding

chairman, San Francisco journalist Leon Adams, thought it might be possible to get André into the country by working through the University of California. At that time the University's school of enology was embryonic, and just in the first phase of building a base of expertise. Since Leon Bonnet's retirement they were bereft of professors who could teach enology, so Adams obtained affidavits on André's behalf from *Wines & Vines* editor Horatio F. Stoll and University of California professor William V. Creuss. But just when it looked like André would be allowed to immigrate, the process foundered in red tape again.

Finally, de Latour contacted an old friend, U.S. Senator Hiram Johnson. Shortly thereafter, André received a telegram from Senator Johnson advising him to contact the U.S. embassy in Paris. His visa had been granted.

Georges de Latour returned to California, leaving the Marquis de Pins to organize the Tchelistcheffs' journey. André and his wife, Alexandria, with their young son, Dmitri, embarked on the glamorous ocean liner *Ile de France* for a seven-day voyage to New York, traveling first-class in a luxurious suite. They arrived in New York on September 21, 1938, then boarded a train for San Francisco.

Georges and Fernande de Latour welcomed their new enologist — and his promise of a bright future — with typical high style. One splendid

San Francisco morning (the city normally sees its finest weather in September) the sleek de Latour Cadillac pulled up to collect him, and he rode with his new employer through a strange volcanic landscape (how different it was from the weathered marine geology of France!) to the quiet little coastal valley that would be his home for fifty-six years.

His new life was inaugurated with a California feast of crawfish and trout (both from the stream running through the property) and ring-necked pheasant also raised on the estate. There were flowers on the table from the Beaulieu gardens, but the centerpiece was one of Madame de Latour's hand-painted French porcelain bowls piled high with the estate's luscious strawberries. Georges raided his cellar for Beaulieu Vineyard wines that he hoped would impress the knowledgeable young man. Among them were a 1918 white wine called Chablis; a Pinot Noir, labeled Burgundy, from the same vintage, and Cabernet Sauvignon 1919. The wines were a little coarse by French standards, André recalled later, but the high-toned beauty of the fruit was astonishing. With fruit of that quality to begin with, he would face merely technical challenges. As André held his glass of Beaulieu Cabernet Sauvignon to the light, the future of California wine glimmered in its ruby depths.

CHAPTER SIX

Golden Years

With André Tchelistcheff's arrival, most of the pieces of the Beaulieu Vineyard picture were in place. Georges and Fernande de Latour had struggled to build their business on a firm foundation and position it perfectly. The culminating element of the de Latour dream would be wines that were indisputably among the best in the world. That was the challenge awaiting André Tchelistcheff in Rutherford.

That first day at Beaulieu, after lunch, de Latour took him down the drive and across the county road to the winery. From the first moment inside the cavernous, dimly-lit building, André had to fight despair. His nose told him what he would later confirm by analysis: the winery was not sanitary, spoilage bacteria were everywhere, the cooperage was in bad shape. A winery of equivalent stature in Bordeaux would be clean and tidy. By comparison, this was an embarrassing mess.

Proudly, even with a degree of arrogance, Georges de Latour offered samples of all the wines. There were some sweet monstrosities, fortified with brandy from the still at the Oakville ranch. There were dreadful white wines, some of them sweet as well as oxidized. There were also various reds, most of them dry, and although the quality of the fruit came through in some instances, many of the wines showed the effects of overripeness, hot fermentation, bad cooperage, failure to top-up barrels, and other fundamental processing errors. Yet there were also a few wines — the dry white called Chablis which had impressed André at lunch, and a sumptuous red blend called Burgundy — that were close to what he had hoped to find. He instinctively disliked the notion of using the names of noble European appellations for generic labeling. However, he understood that de Latour was commercially shrewd. "I accepted it with the bleeding of my heart," he said later, "but it was a necessity."

Finally, he encountered something really outstanding. De Latour presented a deep garnet wine that André could smell before he took the glass. It was Cabernet Sauvignon — good Cabernet Sauvignon, at that. It was still young, that much was obvious from its purplish hue. Yet it was remarkably round and smooth on the palate, and it had real structure — a beginning, a middle, and a long finish. The grapes had been extremely ripe by French standards; the aromas and flavors were extraordinarily intense, even rich. And, of course, the alcohol level was higher than typical Bordeaux. But the fruit was clear and bright, with no trace of raisining, meaning that the grapes had been picked at just the right time for that particular vineyard. There was no trace of the tell-tale hotness that comes with overripeness. Most interesting of all, André could tell that this fine Cabernet had been aged in real *barriques.*

The old man was watching him. "It's very good," said André. The old man beamed.

"It's the best wine we've ever made," he said. "Moreover, it shows what is possible. I want all of my wines to be that good. That's why I have brought you here, Mr. Tchelistcheff."

The wine had that intense Cabernet character that would make BV vineyards #1 and #2 famous. It had been reposing in oak barrels for nearly two years, but rather than being overpowered with the taste of wood, it had only become rounder and more supple. The most intriguing thing about the wine was a whiff of clean dirt with a high-toned note something like pencil shavings. André recognized it as the expression of a distinctive *terroir* — the very fragrance of Rutherford. To describe it, he would later coin the term "Rutherford dust."

At one point during that long afternoon in the cellar, Joseph Ponti came in from the vineyard to meet the new enologist. There was tension between the two men immediately, but Georges de Latour smoothed it over with a pep talk about teamwork and the shining future. Near the end of the day, André was finally shown his new laboratory and suffered another shock: it was nothing more than a closet.

The next morning he requested a complete inventory and samples of all the Beaulieu wines. It took him three weeks to run chemical and microbiological analyses, but when it was done he knew what he was dealing with.

There were problems, indeed, but nothing insurmountable. What was needed, he told Georges de Latour and superintendent Ponti, could be summed up in one word: sanitation. In particular, that meant replacing the old cooperage, which was decayed to the point of being a breeding ground for spoilage microbes, and replacing copper and iron valves and hose fittings with brass and, eventually, stainless steel.

He approved of de Latour's practice of fermenting and storing different grape varieties and vineyard lots separately, but he insisted that the selection had to be more rigorous. Already the very best lots of wine — particularly the Cabernet Sauvignon from the home vineyard — were reserved for the private use of the family. This "private reserve" cuvée, André told his new employer, should be expanded and defined as the pinnacle of the Beaulieu brand rather than being a closely-guarded family secret. The private reserve lots should be aged in small oak barrels, he said, and further aged in bottles before being presented to the world as the crowning jewel of BV's full line.

André was not surprised when the 1936 Cabernet Sauvignon, made by Georges de Latour and Joseph Ponti under the scientific supervision of Professor Bonnet, took a Gold Medal (one of four golds awarded BV) at the 1939 Golden Gate International Exposition in San Francisco. But even he had to be impressed when it subsequently commanded the unprecedented price of $1.50 a bottle.

THE GENESIS OF PRIVATE RESERVE

Georges de Latour had known for a long time that Cabernet Sauvignon was Rutherford's strong suit. For years it had been his habit to regularly taste all the wines in his cellar. He always focused on the best wines, and the best wines were always Cabernet. De Latour took pleasure in showing his best wines to guests at Beaulieu, and was not above subjecting them to impromptu blind tastings. Joseph Ponti recalled being present when de Latour poured his '36 Cabernet next to Château Mouton Rothschild for some San Francisco bankers; to his great and obvious satisfaction, they preferred the Beaulieu wine.

There are many stories about the introduction of Private Reserve. The version generally accepted by historians is the one Hélène de Pins told Legh Knowles in the early 1960s:

One evening in 1939 the de Latours were gathered in their house on Scott Street in San Francisco. As Hélène de Latour recalled, her father came in with a bottle of wine in his hands. He said, "I'm glad you're all here, because I want you to taste this wine. I really think that it could be the making of our reputation." Hélène noticed a tone of finality in her father's voice, and thought he looked unduly tired.

He opened the bottle. A lovely perfume of Cabernet Sauvignon pervaded the room. They all tasted the wine and marveled at its beauty. According to Mme de Latour, it was manager Nino Fabbrini who subsequently named the wine "Georges de Latour Private Reserve." It was a masterstroke of marketing that gave California wine its first and most enduring icon. Indeed, that was Fabbrini's finest hour.

De Latour's alliance with the New York distributor Park & Tilford should have been triumphant, but instead came close to putting BV out of business. In 1937 he contracted to deliver 25,000 cases of estate-bottled wine yearly, but the first carloads sent to New York were flawed. They were returned in 1938, just in time to be received by André Tchelistcheff, who recalled later that "carloads of wine…had to be dumped…. There was refermentation in the bottle, there was a breakdown of mineral salts in the bottle, wines murky, muddy in the glass." The most pervasive problem was high volatile acidity. "It was a tragedy," said André.

Georges and Fernande de Latour were mortified. It was a replay of the debacle a few years earlier, but more dire. This time, there was no scapegoat, no one to sue, no one to fire. The truth was simple: While they had invested money in buying more vineyards and planting them with noble grape varieties, the winemaking facilities were still below standard. Characteristically, their response was to meet the problem head-on, and the money they subsequently invested in upgrading the winemaking facilities ultimately lifted BV from one of the "Big Four" Napa Valley wine producers to a clear first place. New equipment was installed, and all flawed wines (reportedly fifty percent of the inventory) were sold off. André said bluntly, "I liquidated all this wine of old inventory and sent it to the distillery."

Georges de Latour didn't live to see how his final efforts propelled Beaulieu Vineyard to the pinnacle of American wine. The haunting fatigue his daughter had noticed the night he presented his finest wine became a serious illness. By the time cancer was diagnosed, it was too late. After a brief struggle, he passed away in the family home at 2650 Scott Street in San Francisco, surrounded by Fernande and their children, Hélène and Richard, on February 28, 1940.

PASSING ON THE LEGACY

Georges de Latour was eighty-four when he died. His requiem mass, at the Church of Notre Dame des Victoires — the church in which he and Fernande were married — was attended by more than 500 people. Among the pallbearers were Mayor Rossi, Rear Adm. Arthur J. Hepburn, Rear Adm. Alexander S. Halstead (retired); Roger Gaucheron; John Daniels, Jr.; L.M. Fabbrini; Herman Wente; and Aldo Fabbrini. Archbishop Mitty gave the benediction, and Los Angeles Archbishop John Cantwell was also present.

A *San Francisco Examiner* columnist ("Getting Around with Cholly") wrote, "With the passing of Georges de Latour, one more link which joins the brusque, rather ruthless manners of today with the courtly old-fashioned way of doing things is severed. For this esteemed and highly respected Frenchman was truly a gentleman of the 'old school.' None who ever came into contact with him, either in a business way or as a guest, but will retain the impression of *gentility*."

Admiringly, he added that Georges de Latour "could quote page after page from Racine, Corneille and Molière!"

An obituary in the *Examiner* noted that he "played a notable part in molding the San Francisco we know and love today, in the formative period of its civic character."

Fernande de Latour immediately stepped into her husband's role (which she had in any case shared from the beginning), joining the fabled ranks of legendary vintner-widows such as Mmes Cliquot and Pommery. She was ably assisted by Nino Fabbrini. They never got along really well, and she kept him in his place — "She's the queen, and I'm the prime minister," joked Fabbrini — but they made a good management team. She got along better on a personal level with André Tchelistcheff; others recall that they were open and comfortable together, if somewhat formal in the Old World style. Eventually the de Latours' daughter, Hélène de Pins, assumed control of the company after her mother's death in 1952, and ran it until 1969. In all, Beaulieu Vineyard was run by women for twenty-nine years.

Throughout the 40s, BV wines were wines of state. Thanks to the consistent high quality of the wines produced by André Tchelistcheff and his team, BV supplied wines for dinners and receptions honoring some of the great people of the age. Mme de Latour was one of the most influential business people in the West, with good connections in Sacramento and Washington, not to mention the Catholic Church. Her network spread to Europe as well. In the postwar period, traveling dignitaries like Winston Churchill, and ambassadors from Denmark, Monaco, England, and France gave Beaulieu the aura of a United Nations retreat in the Napa Valley.

In fact, the de Pins were part of the French aristocracy. Mme de Latour made good use of the family's French connections in 1949, when she firmly established BV's lasting reputation by taking her best wines to Paris and presenting them both formally and informally. She and the de Pins took up residence in the fashionable Hotel George V, a high-society address, and methodically made sure that all the leading restaurateurs and wine dealers tasted BV wines in the most agreeable

circumstances. Thus, in high style BV cemented its international reputation, the first California winery to do so.

The big white house at Beaulieu continued to welcome distinguished visitors from around the world. Each morning the Beaulieu domestic staff reported to Fernande in her bedroom. Their Japanese chef, Roy Hiroaka, would propose a menu. She would agree or disagree, and they would refine the meal together. The standby dish for luncheons was a codfish omelette with potatoes. The slow-simmered stew was another pillar of Beaulieu cuisine. According to Dagmar, "The criterion for hiring a cook was if the cook could make a proper omelette and a proper stew."

Arriving guests would be greeted with a glass of Pommery Champagne. They strolled the gardens and the long, shaded arbor, often catching their own trout and crayfish for dinner from the large stone pools along the stream just above the bridge, or choosing the evening's pheasant from the estate's bird run. On cool evenings they gathered at the fine old table by the fireplace in the high-ceilinged dining room. Luncheon was often served by the fountain, and Dagmar de Pins Sullivan recalls lavish brunches at streamside, with men in morning coats and ladies in fabulous hats. Wherever they were served, the de Latour family and their guests ate from Mme de Latour's splendid Luneville porcelain tableware with the distinctive hand-painted rooster motif. And they drank Beaulieu Vineyard wines from a cellar with a depth of vintages unequalled in America.

Only a generation earlier, California wines had been snubbed by

MARQUISE HÉLÈNE DE
PINS AND MARQUIS
GALCERAND DE PINS
AND IN THE BEAULIEU
GARDEN, 1955

opposite:
GALCERAND AND
HÉLÈNE IN EUROPE,
1954

President McKinley during a visit to San Francisco, where he ordered French wine for a banquet feting local supporters. Now, the government had an American wine they could be proud to serve on great occasions. The White House poured BV wines at dinners given for Generals Dwight D. Eisenhower and Douglas MacArthur in New York. General Charles de Gaulle drank Beaulieu Beaurosé at a Waldorf Astoria luncheon. The French Foreign Minister in San Francisco poured Beaulieu Chablis at a dinner honoring British diplomat Sir Anthony Eden. And Winston S. Churchill was served Georges de Latour Private Reserve at a banquet in his honor at the Waldorf Astoria.

Fernande de Latour continued to build the Beaulieu Vineyard empire as well. Her husband had always admired the Martin Stelling, Jr. property in Rutherford, and when ninety acres became available in 1943, she acted swiftly to make it BV#4. She also demonstrated skill in maintaining the dynamic management machine built by Georges de Latour in the years before his death. When Nino Fabbrini passed away in 1946, she hired his brother Aldo; he managed BV until his retirement in 1962.

Meanwhile, André Tchelistcheff perceived a dire need for sound enological practice throughout California. His first impression of Napa Valley viticulture had been extremely negative, and he continued to be appalled by the "primitiveness" of the way wine was being made in California. "Do you know, my dear sir," he once asked a journalist rhetorically, "that when I came to California nobody in the industry believed malolactic fermentation, as a phenomenon, even existed?" His 1947 paper on malolactic fermentation in California red wines was the first published report on the subject.

Although his primary concern was Beaulieu, André consulted for Charles Krug, Inglenook, Louis Martini, Sebastiani, Buena Vista, and other wineries. In 1947 (with Fernande's blessing) he opened the Napa Valley Enological Research Laboratory in St. Helena. Below the big sign on the front door was another, smaller sign that said, Napa Valley Enological Center. That was a coalition of the valley's young men who worked together on technical problems affecting the valley's wine-producing community. Members included Peter and Robert Mondavi, Louis P. Martini, August Sebastiani, John Daniel, Lee Stewart, and several others.

Part of the impetus for the NVEC was a requirement by the Bank of America, which at that time had financial control of virtually all Napa Valley wineries, that each winery show proof of the soundness of its wines on a monthly basis. It turned out to be a blessing in disguise by effectively making quality control a community concern, thereby strengthening the Napa Valley wine community at its core during a rapid and therefore vulnerable phase in its evolution. The NVEC evolved over the years into the Napa Valley Technical Group, which played a major role in the subsequent rise of the valley's fortunes. The group is still active today, with more than 200 members, and it remains a vital aspect of Napa Valley wine.

Unfortunately, Joseph Ponti and André Tchelistcheff didn't get along all that well. They came from two different worlds and points of view. André never spoke for the record about Ponti, but Ponti said he always felt that the Russian enologist was arrogant. Ponti respected André's credentials and gave grudging respect to some of his practices, yet couldn't help resenting that whatever the enologist did got automatic approval, while the Italian immigrant who had pulled himself up by his bootstraps was always second-guessed.

FERNANDE DE LATOUR AND ANDRÉ TCHELISTCHEFF PULLING A NEW WINE SAMPLE FROM AN AGING VAT IN THE BV CELLAR, 1948

Having brought the winery's sanitation issues under control, André faced the biggest winemaking challenge of the time: fresh white wines. Clearly, there was a big market for white wines, but the usual whites available to consumers were dull, oxidized wines that "turned" early. Most winemakers at the time dreamed of producing crisp, dry whites comparable to French Chablis and Muscadet.

André applied science to the problem. He built a cold room, like a giant walk-in refrigerator, for fermenting white wines. The low temperature (about 65 degrees F) captured the fruit and allowed the sugar to convert into alcohol without cooking off the delicacy. He also made sure the wine wasn't inadvertently oxidized on its path through the winery. This was standard practice in France, but new to California.

Ponti had also attacked the problem. His solution was on a smaller scale and probably not adequate, but it demonstrated yet again his natural capability and an aptitude for practical engineering. He designed and built a temperature-controlled vat, long before the advent of glycol-jacketed stainless steel tanks became standard equipment. This was a forerunner of modern technology that came right out of Ponti's head. His invention was a concrete tank with a wooden vessel inside it. By filling the concrete tank with ice he cooled the liner, and the wine inside the liner.

Ponti was, indeed, "an intelligent fellow" who had a good basic education and spoke several languages fluently. Yet he was hampered by the lack of a formal education. In a world increasingly dominated by institutions and credentials he was undervalued. From our viewpoint in the present we can see that Joseph J. Ponti had a great deal to do with the success of Beaulieu Vineyard, but at the time his contributions were apparently taken for granted.

Years later he said in an interview that his relationship with André Tchelistcheff was uneasy and often competitive. "I and he never did agree very much. After all, I was the winemaker. If he was going to interfere, I would tell him to get away from me…. He is a peculiar fellow, you know. If he does something that succeeds, he blows up, he thinks there's nothing like him, see."

SURVIVING A
CONFLAGRATION

One afternoon in 1947, Joseph Ponti awoke from a nap in a rustic room at Adams Spring in Lake County. He had arrived earlier that day, and after checking in had gone to his room in a small cottage to lie down before dinner.

It was the first vacation he'd taken in all his time at Beaulieu. He felt relaxed and hungry, and enjoyed a rare sense of ease all the way from his room to the main lodge. In the lobby he spotted a couple of French businessmen from San Francisco, who invited him to have a drink before dinner. But before he could even sit down one of the young women who worked in the dining room came up to him. "We've had several calls from Rutherford," she said. "They've been wanting to get you for quite a while."

Immediately worried, Ponti went to the phone and the woman connected him. The Marquis de Pins answered, in French.

"Ponti, it's burning!"

"What's burning?"

"The winery is on fire."

Ponti rushed back to his room and threw everything back into his valise. On his way out to the car, he remembered that his gas tank was low.

Wartime gas rationing was till in effect, and although they had gas at Beaulieu he always tried to get by on as little as possible. The faster he drove, the more he would use — but by coasting on the hills, Ponti figured, he could make it back in good time with gas to spare.

As he entered the Napa Valley north of Calistoga, he could see black smoke billowing into the sky from Rutherford. By the time he got there, all he could do was join the crowd and watch as the fire burned itself out. André Tchellistchef looked on, too, grimly smoking a cigarette.

Ponti's nephew, Louis Tonella, was the chief of the Rutherford Volunteer Fire Department from 1945–1955. He was in his family's store at the crossroads, next door to the winery, when the fire started. He recalls smelling smoke, and then the alarm siren wailed. "It was early afternoon. Somebody smelled smoke, and first thing we know the roof of the winery was on fire. Somebody pulled the siren. Napa and St. Helena sent their trucks, but really all we could do was squirt water over the top. Nobody had a ladder truck. Luckily, nobody was injured — we all just stayed outside and squirted water. When we knocked it down we'd open the doors and put water in, late in the day, but they let it burn. We had it out about midnight. But the tanks burst — when we opened up the back door a flood of wine about three feet deep came out. People came from all over the valley to watch that fire."

The old stone section of the original Seneca Ewer winery was spared, and with it the superb Cabernet Sauvignon wines meant for the Georges de Latour Private Reserve. So was the new fermentation room. But the middle of the winery, containing about 600,000 gallons of wine, was totally destroyed.

Nobody was ever able to say for sure what caused the fire, but there was speculation. One reasonable theory had to do with Fred Ewer and his friends, who used to sit on top of the winery through long summer twilights, drinking and playing cards. Inevitably there was some broken glass scattered about on the roof from that time. A hot sun hitting broken glass just right can start a fire; Ponti, for one, believed that was the likeliest explanation for how the fire started.

"BV had quite a fire protection," noted Chief Tonella. "There was a reservoir, and hydrants, and they had fire doors. That kept it confined to that one room. Otherwise it would have been worse." The wine remaining in the

tanks was ruined — tainted by smoke and diluted with sooty water. It was sold off for distilling. In a gesture that has become traditional in the competitive but mutually supportive Napa Valley wine industry, neighboring wineries offered wines to make up the loss and help the company make it through until more wine could be produced.

This generosity fulfilled a nice historical symmetry: Georges de Latour had helped the California wine industry survive phylloxera and Prohibition. Now, the Napa Valley wine community came together to lend a hand to the de Latours.

The 1947 growing season had been nearly perfect, yielding one of the finest of all Georges de Latour Private Reserves. When it was tasted in London in July, 1999, the '47 was fully alive, with an elegant silkiness on the palate and a clear note of Rutherford dust in the finish. Unfortunately, some 10,000 gallons of it had to be bottled as Rutherford Cabernet to compensate for the fire loss.

THE FINE
FIFTIES

The 1950s were a golden time for California wine, and for Beaulieu in particular. The BV cellars were increasingly a magnet for young talent, such as a

young chemist named Joseph Heitz who came aboard in the spring of 1951. A string of excellent vintages further consolidated the reputation of Georges de Latour Private Reserve, which found an unprecedented market. In the surge of new prosperity following World War II, wine enjoyed increasing popularity in the middle class. A generation of young people had been exposed to wine as a daily fact of life during military service in Europe. Serving wine with dinner thus began to seem like a normal thing to do, and an absolute necessity for anyone wishing to display a note of Continental sophistication.

New profits attracted attention from corporations, and there was a wave of winery buyouts. As sales of California wine went on to triple in the late 50s and early 60s (thereafter stalled by a flood of inexpensive imports subsidized by European governments), there was increasing interest from large corporations. BV always entertained offers, but Mme de Latour consistently refused to sell. Nor did she allow BV to expand radically beyond the parameters of steady growth. That policy helped protect the quality of BV wines, and the integrity of the brand.

Fernande de Latour passed away peacefully on October 12, 1951. Under her administration Beaulieu had consolidated its reputation as California's first world-class winery, with some 600 acres of vines in four choice parcels in the very heart of Napa Valley.

MADAME FERNANDE DE LATOUR, C.1950

Hélène de Latour (now Marquise de Pins) became president of BV. Despite the grief in Rutherford, Beaulieu's image continued to gain luster. President Truman served BV Burgundy and Rhine Wine to Queen Juliana of the Netherlands at the Carlton Hotel, Washington, D.C. Two days later, New York mayor La Guardia presented Queen Juliana the Georges de Latour Private Reserve 1942 (a particularly elegant vintage) at a luncheon in her honor.

Hélène de Pins preserved the BV policy of rejecting corporate suitors and protecting the family proprietorship. Yet she had a somewhat less avid taste for business than her mother (while her husband, the Marquis de Pins, had no interest in being in California whatsoever), and thus she relied more than Mme de Latour on the BV managers.

From top to bottom it was an energetic and capable crew. In addition to André Tchelistcheff and Joseph Ponti, the winery was run by a superior team that prided itself on competence and efficiency. Joseph Heitz plunged into the role of André's understudy, learning the nuts and bolts of winemaking that he would later apply to his own Heitz Cellar wines — including Martha's Vineyard Cabernet Sauvignon, perhaps the most famous California wine after Georges de Latour Private Reserve. The de Latour family's long-standing policy of hiring eager immigrants continued to pay off; the BV cellar was full of young, vigorous men whose character and commitment more than made up for any lack of previous winery experience.

Just before Christmas in 1954 a young man from Holland arrived in the Napa Valley. Theo Rosenbrand was just thirty-one and had no fixed career plans except that he wanted to get ahead somehow. He had a friend working in the BV cellar, and arrangements were made for him to stay in a guest room at Beaulieu.

On Christmas morning one of the cellar workers came over from the winery to see how Theo was doing and wish him a merry Christmas. It was Joe Heitz, "the first American I met after coming from Europe," as Theo recalled. The two hit it off, and kept in touch. Theo got a job in St. Helena making copies of antiques in hydro-stone and plaster. In July, 1956 he got a call from his friend Joe Heitz, by then the BV plant manager, saying there was a job available in the winery that would pay twenty-five cents more than Theo was making in the antique shop, plus benefits. "André interviewed me in his office," recalls Theo. "I had an accent and so did he, and I didn't understand one damn word he said. But I must have said yes and no at the right time, because they hired me." The starting wage was $1.50 an hour.

ANDRÉ TCHELISTCHEFF THIEVING OUT A SAMPLE OF THE 1950 BV CHABLIS FROM A 350 LITER TONNEAUX, 1951

Theo went to work for cellar foreman Ernest Digardi, pulling hoses and doing pump-overs. Before long he was helping keep records and direct traffic. When Digardi retired in 1964, André made Theo Rosenbrand the cellar foreman. His wife also took a job at BV, handling taxes, payroll, and other administrative tasks. One of her jobs was filling out the government forms for bulk shipping; Beaulieu was still sending some wine out in barrels for bottling by distributors in Chicago and New York — but by this time, the distributors were owned by BV.

When Mrs. Rosenbrand became pregnant with their first child in July, 1958, a young woman from St. Helena named Dorothy Andrew took her place. Dorothy's husband was the first principal of Robert Louis Stevenson School in St. Helena. They had four children, and had just moved to Napa Valley the previous year. Dorothy didn't feel quite comfortable in St. Helena.

"It was a closed town," she recalls, adding, "It still is." She sensed resentment in the community that her husband had been brought from outside (they'd been living in the Sierra foothills) to open the school. She even felt that they resented their four children. Dorothy worked part-time at the high school, and she also worked with the Cub Scouts, the Girl Scouts, 4-H, and the Rainbow Girls (a church group). But she never felt that the family was really accepted by the St. Helenans.

That, she recalled later, "made it easier, in a way, when everything turned upside down" — a reference to a new romance with a certain Russian-born enologist that simmered with increasing vigor for several years.

Throughout the 1950s BV general manager Aldo Fabbrini, with the confidence of the de Pins and Sullivan families, continued to keep BV ahead of the competition. A salient example is the introduction in 1956 of an innovation which has since become commonplace: the educational back label. It first appeared on a small bottling (only several thousand cases) of BV "Beaufort" Pinot Chardonnay, of which BV's fifteen acres were, incredibly, the largest planting in the valley. A masterful piece of gentle propaganda, it conveyed an impression that the Beaulieu Chardonnay vines were a direct extension of the "famed White Burgundies of France," adding that Chardonnay grown on the Beaulieu estate produced a delightful wine, "fragrant and smooth, with a flavor reminiscent of still Champagne." Fabbrini also continued his brother's and Mme de Latour's policy of aggressively placing BV wines on high-profile restaurant and hotel wine lists. BV continued its

unofficial role as the winery of state. On March 24, 1959, Queen Elizabeth and Prince Phillip were served Georges de Latour Private Reserve at a Pan American Union dinner hosted by U.S. Secretary of State John Foster Dulles.

Also in that year, the cellar crew acquired another eager immigrant, Miljenko "Mike" Grgich. Joining the throng of Tchelistcheff protégés, Mike Grgich honed his skills for nine years before going to Château Montelena as a winemaker/partner in 1968. Subsequently, one of his wines, the Château Montelena Chardonnay '73, dominated French competitors in the famous Academie du Vin Paris Tasting of 1976. The yeast that Grgich used to ferment that wine was a special slow-fermenting strain developed by the Institut Pasteur in Paris; he had been introduced to it several years earlier by André Tchelistcheff in the BV cellars.

Between 1959 and 1962, production increased from 65,000 to 85,000 cases, and Fabbrini's crack team easily sold every drop. In that atmosphere of success it was easy for André Tchelistcheff to convince Mme de Pins to realize his long-standing dream of a cool-climate vineyard. BV#5, 160 acres in the Carneros district, was purchased in 1962 and immediately planted with Pinot Noir and Chardonnay.

CHECKING SPARKLING
WINE FOR CLARITY
AFTER RIDDLING IN
THE BV CELLAR, 1950S

opposite:
BV BOTTLING LINE,
WITH MULTI-SPOUT
HAND FILLER, 1950S

RACKING WINE OUT
OF AMERICAN OAK
BARRELS AND
CLEANING THEM
FOR REFILLING,
1950S

THE STEAMY
SIXTIES

*I*n 1962 another memorable character entered the BV story, when the Marquise de Pins hired an ex-trumpet player who had found a second career in the wine industry. He would prove to be a true friend of the de Latours and the Beaulieu brand.

In the upbeat years following Repeal, a new generation of happy social drinkers had enjoyed their cocktails and wines to the popular sounds of big bands on the radio. One of the most popular was the Glen Miller Orchestra. Revelers hearing Miller's outfit at a nightspot like the Stork Club in

Manhattan swung to the sounds of a cool young trumpeter named Legh Knowles playing "In the Mood," "Moonlight Serenade," and "Tuxedo Junction." Knowles joined the Miller band in 1939 and made 123 records with them. He also performed with Charlie Spivak, Red Norvo, and Mildred Bailey.

He later said that Glenn Miller was a big influence on his notion of professionalism. "Glenn was absolutely the greatest executive I ever worked for. He was, no question, brilliant. Made you learn. He never said you played well. He said, 'I pay you to play well. I don't pay you to make mistakes. I pay you to play perfectly.' That's hard to hear, but boy, that's right."

Knowles joined the U.S. Air Force in 1941. After the war, he went to work for the Wine Advisory Board, a California lobbying group based in Washington, D.C. "I didn't know anything about wine," he said later. "But they wanted someone who could stand up before large crowds, and I'd done a lot of that."

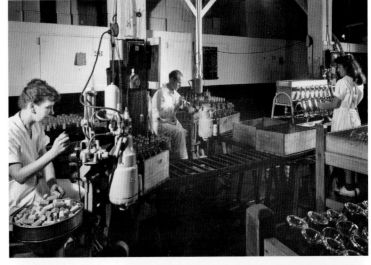

From the Wine Advisory Board he went into the private sector, first with Taylor Wine Co. and then with Ernest and Julio Gallo. He proved himself in the tough Cincinnati market, increasing Gallo's sales there dramatically, and was promoted to national accounts.

In 1962, the largest-selling wine in America was white Port, and that was Gallo's main product. It was more of a commodity beverage than a wine; Legh Knowles felt he had hit a dead end at Gallo. He wanted to go into the premium wine business, but at that time the Federal Trade Commission was making expansion difficult and top-level jobs in the wine industry were scarce. Legh's wife was ill, too, so they decided that he would return to the East Coast to work

MARQUISE HÉLÈNE DE
PINS IN THE BV
GARDENS, LATE 1950S

opposite:
MARQUIS GALCERAND
DE PINS AND
MARQUISE HÉLÈNE DE
PINS TASTING WINE IN
THE BV CELLAR, C.1956

for a large company such as Zenith. On a whim, he wrote to Hélène de Pins. He told her that from his first day in the wine business he had admired BV wine and all that it stood for, and that he thought he could contribute to the business.

Mme de Pins invited him to a board meeting at BV's offices on California Street in San Francisco. BV's current sales manager, Aldo Fabbrini, was not present; a decision had been made that it was time to replace him. A short time after the meeting, Legh Knowles was hired as sales manager.

He recalled later that he thought Mme de Pins had hired him on a hunch. "I don't know what it was with her, but she thought I could do some good. I had a feeling she didn't have confidence in her sales management." He signed a one-year contract, but he told her he needed more money. At the end of one year she gave him a fat bonus — and he gave half of it back.

One of Knowles's first big challenges was distribution. Park & Tilford had been acquired by Schenley, which also owned Cresta Blanca Winery. The head of Schenley, Lewis R. Rosentiel, saw BV as competing with Cresta Blanca. Word reached BV that Rosentiel had allegedly said, "What the hell is that Beaulieu? I'll bury that Beaulieu." Furious, Mme de Pins pulled BV from the Park & Tilford contract, leaving it up to Legh Knowles to find new distribution. That wasn't easy — "Nobody was even interested in wine in 1962," he said — but he managed to do it.

A big part of Legh Knowles's success was his ability to cut to the chase. When the white wine boom arrived, he said, "You know what that is? That's a *cold* wine syndrome, not a *white* wine syndrome." And BV's market-leading dry, crisp whites were right on target.

Unlike Ponti, Legh hit it off with André Tchelistcheff. One of the things they agreed on was that the BV product line should be compacted. To feed its extensive national distribution network, taking into account a range of regional markets and tastes, BV produced what the trade called "a complete line" of wines, including generic and varietal table wines, dessert wines, and even sparkling wines. Initially, the main reason for so many different products was that BV meant different things to people in different markets. The winery's largest-selling wine in New York was Burgundy. In Cleveland, it was Dry Sauterne (which was Semillon). Chicagoans favored Port, Milwaukeans Johannesburg Riesling. Las Vegas drank Rosé, and Los Angeles Chablis.

For years, as often as he could without pushing things too far, Tchelistcheff had urged Mme de Latour and the company's other directors to narrow the range of wines and concentrate on a few top-level wines, after the example of the great French châteaux that Georges de Latour had wanted to emulate. "With thirty wines to take care of," he said, "I am producing little starlets when I should produce only great stars."

Legh Knowles listened, and agreed. When he arrived, they were selling forty different products; within a few years they were focusing on ten.

Of course, the biggest-selling BV wine in sophisticated San Francisco was Cabernet Sauvignon. That was the wine that attracted Legh to BV, and his enthusiasm for the varietal never waned. In an interview after his retirement he summed up his attitude: If someone were to ask him what he would do now, he said, "I'd be the King of Cabernet. I'd have Cabernet

from Washington, Oregon, Mendocino, Petaluma, Napa, Tepusquet. I would have a million cases, and I would sell the Cabernet from three dollars a bottle to three hundred dollars a bottle. But I'd be working with one grape."

The winery became a rather steamy place during the sixties. Dorothy, the administrative secretary who had replaced Theo Rosenbrand's wife and become part of the BV family, had her office behind the tasting room, on the north side of the building, with a window that faced the grape scale. During harvest, she would often glance out the window to see one of her bosses, the handsome Russian winemaker, talking with growers while their grapes were weighed.

André was married, too (to his second wife), and had two sons. Neither he nor Dorothy, however, had the kind of chemistry with their mates that they felt with each other. Knowing what kind of damage they could do made them reluctant to acknowledge the attraction, but eventually it became obvious to everyone in the winery that something was going on. By the late sixties André and Dorothy had reached the point of no return.

In 1968, as Dorothy puts it, "I got a divorce and he got a divorce, and St. Helena tipped on its side." People still recall the scandal (which was only eclipsed a decade later when Robert Mondavi and Margrit Biever divorced their spouses to marry each other). André was sixty-seven; Dorothy, forty-four. Dorothy had never paid any attention to wine before moving to the Napa Valley, but now she devoted herself to learning about it.

In the winter of '68, after his "baby wines" were safely tucked into barrels, André took Dorothy to Paris. They stayed in a little hotel that André remembered from his student days, on the Rue de Rennes near Montparnasse. He knew it had a little elevator with steam pipes that went up the shaft; they requested a room next to the elevator and stayed cozy through the Parisian winter.

Everywhere they went, Dorothy recalls, André was respected, whether he knew the proprietors or not. "Many places we'd go, the owner would be cautious and the door would be open very slightly. Then they'd get to talking, and you could be very sure that some of those old bottles with the mold on them would come out, because they knew that he knew what he was talking about. That was something to see."

BV's enologist had found new happiness — but by that time, BV's

fortunes were waning again. For two decades after Georges de Latour's death, Beaulieu Vineyard had prospered. Gradually, however, it was overtaken by trouble. The company was land-rich while the winery itself was declining. The situation was similar to the bad old days of the 1930s, except that then the problem had been a lack of available capital. Now the problem was an unwillingness to fund necessary upgrades.

By the late 1960s, BV appeared increasingly vulnerable, and purchase offers from large companies increased dramatically as the business world picked up the scent of the coming wine boom. Suitors included Budweiser, Baccardi, and several French wine companies.

Legh handled the interviews. After the Annheuser-Busch interview, he had lunch with Hélène de Latour at the Ritz Old Poodle Dog on Post Street. She said, "I want to ask you something. Would you rather work for them or for me?"

Knowles replied, "For you, Madame de Pins." The offer was rejected.

Then, on June 5, 1969, the Marquise de Pins sold Beaulieu Vineyard after all. "It's a terrible wrench," the Marquise told the *San Francisco Chronicle,* "but circumstances force changes. It is more practical for a big organization to operate in these times."

The circumstances forcing the sale can be summed up in two distressing words: failing business. The property was undervalued; Dagmar Sullivan still cringes at the thought. "We weren't paid as much as we should have been," she said in 1999. "Not that it was in as good shape as it is now, but I know now that these people get a hundred million dollars like it was five dollars. But I have never crossed the threshold of the winery since. It makes me too sad. I wish it hadn't happened."

Joseph Ponti was still in bed early one morning when the phone rang. It was Hélène. "Ponti," she said, "I did it. I sold out."

"What? You sold Beaulieu?"

"Not the homeplace," she said. "But everything else."

Ponti wasn't sure he understood. "Do you remember when we had lunch and your father was still living, and he wanted you to promise that if he ever died you wouldn't sell Beaulieu?"

"I remember."

"Well, I just wanted to remind you," said Ponti.

"No," said Hélène. "I didn't sell Beaulieu."

When the Marquise and Dagmar announced to Otto Gramlow and Legh Knowles that they had sold BV, Legh recalls, they cried.

CHAPTER SEVEN

A New Era

*A*s the American middle class awoke to the pleasures of table wine in the late 1960s, a global beverage company named Heublein, Inc. kept pace by sending an acquisition team from its home base in Hartford, Connecticut, to the Napa Valley. Best known for its white spirits brands, primarily Smirnoff Vodka and Gilbey's Gin, Heublein had never been a wine producer before, although it imported more than a million gallons of wine annually under such brands as Lancers and Harvey's.

In 1968 the company's newly created fine wines division purchased United Vintners, the second-largest seller of wine products in the country. Its two major brands were Italian Swiss Colony and Inglenook (acquired from the John Daniels family in 1964), among others. Almost immediately, the Federal Trade Commission filed an antitrust suit alleging that the size and commercial influence of Italian Swiss Colony effectively restricted free trade in the wine market and thus violated antitrust laws. The FTC suit ground along in the courts for the better part of a decade before the complaint was dismissed in 1980. Meanwhile, both Italian Swiss Colony and Inglenook were seriously compromised.

Heublein also sent a team to Beaulieu, consisting of vice president Stuart Watson and an ambitious young executive named Andy Beckstoffer. They met quietly with Walter Sullivan and purchased BV for about $8 million — a fraction of what it would be worth even a few years later — before any of the employees knew what was happening. Then Watson flew back to Hartford, leaving Beckstoffer in charge. Beaulieu was purchased directly by Heublein to become part of the spirits division of the company, and was therefore not involved in the FTC antitrust litigation. While the wine division spiraled toward doom, BV would prosper.

What Heublein bought was the BV brand, the winery and its inventory, the BV distributing company, and — the greatest prize — the BV vineyards. The de Pins–Sullivan family kept the original de Latour residential estate and 123 acres of vines. Hélène de Pins was named Honorary Chairman of the Board, and her son-in-law, San Francisco realtor Walter Sullivan, became a board member.

The sale had been rather precipitous, and the reasoning behind it uneasy. Madame de Pins was no longer interested in running a winery, nor were Dagmar and Walter Sullivan. They had been told repeatedly by André and Legh Knowles that BV needed a large infusion of capital, and they were not prepared to make that commitment. Together, they had decided that the proceeds from selling the winery could be invested to help support their intercontinental lifestyle. The sale had happened suddenly, with the feel of a palace coup.

DEALING WITH
NEW REALITIES

*A*ndy Beckstoffer's first job was to explain Heublein's purchase of the
company to André Tchelistcheff. By all subsequent accounts, it was not a
comfortable moment. They met in Beckstoffer's new office, where he went
through a long spiel for the stony-faced Russian. When he was through talking there was a long silence. Then André said, "Talk is cheap. We'll see what
you do."

A recalcitrant winemaker was not Beckstoffer's only problem. "I
quickly realized that we didn't have enough grapes for Inglenook or BV, so I
was asked to form a company to get grapes," he recalls. "That's when we developed the economics of prime varietal vineyards, and then I was asked to
set up a farming company." Vinifera Development Corporation, a subsidiary
of Heublein, was formed in 1970. By 1972, VDC was farming some 3,000
acres (about ten percent of the Napa Valley) and had a long-term grape supply for Inglenook and BV firmly in place.

After overcoming his initial shock at the sale, André tried to put a
good face on it by embracing the promises made by Heublein executives to
purchase more vineyards and land that could be planted to vines. He was

quickly disillusioned. It was a fundamental precept of his European winemaking background that fine wines begin in vineyards that are under the complete control of the château or winery. Thus it was "a terrific shock" to André when the Keig Ranch and BV#3 were turned over to Andy Beckstoffer's Vinifera Development Corporation. And it soon became clear, to his great distress, that Heublein had no plans to purchase more land. He was further upset when the company insisted on buying inferior Cabernet grapes from other vineyards it owned, and blending that fruit into wines from the superb vineyards that Georges de Latour had devoted his life to developing.

At the same time, Beckstoffer clearly perceived that Heublein was more interested in short-term profit than long-term commitment. And it was clear to him that if he could manipulate the situation effectively, BV's viticultural loss would be his gain.

"After everything it took to establish VDC," recalls Beckstoffer, "Heublein said okay, let's sell the company. But I couldn't find a buyer for this not-for-profit company with a union contract. And Heublein couldn't find me a job with them that I wanted to take. So I said, sell me the company." Heublein and Connecticut Mutual Life loaned him the money and he went into business in 1973. Although Beckstoffer went through some tough times in the ensuing years of double-digit inflation, the tale ended happily for him. Beckstoffer Vineyards became the largest independent grower in Napa Valley; the heart of the company is still those original Beaulieu vineyards purchased from Heublein. Beckstoffer knew their true value while Heublein did not.

With the sale of these vineyards to Beckstoffer, André was torn by strong mixed feelings. On one hand, he was disturbed by the shift from family to corporate ownership. He was all too aware that a large company's dedication to the bottom line would likely be at odds with the demands of producing fine wine — chief among them, the correlation between high quality and low production. On the other hand, BV desperately needed an infusion of capital on a scale that only a corporation could provide. Theo Rosenbrand and his cellar crew had become adept at keeping decrepit equipment operating, often wiring or taping parts together just to keep a pump or conveyor working through the end of a shift. If Beckstoffer's promises came true — if Heublein put money into the winery and vineyards without interfering with production standards — then the corporate makeover could be a good thing. André and his staff waited to see how things would play out.

Heublein's moves toward the lucrative generic wine market were inspired by the success that Gallo, California's largest winery, was having with its Hearty Burgundy and other well-made, consistently palatable jug wine. Much of Gallo's success was attributed to a talented, quality control-oriented winemaker named Dr. Richard Peterson. In a stroke of unintended good timing, André Tchelistcheff had lured Peterson to Beaulieu from Gallo just prior to the Heublein takeover.

One day in 1968 the *San Francisco Chronicle* business section ran a photograph of Dr. Peterson next to a paragraph announcing his appointment as Winemaster at BV. In Modesto, Ernest Gallo got a call from his wife, Amelia. When she told him about it, he was furious. He hadn't known that Dick Peterson was looking for another job.

In the new regime, Dr. Peterson was responsible for running the cellar. André's title was technical director. Perhaps it should have been the other

ANDRÉ TCHELISTCHEFF
IN THE LABORATORY AT
BV, EARLY 60S

way around. Peterson had a Ph.D. in agricultural chemistry from UC Berkeley, and his winemaking career so far had been oriented toward producing and bottling huge volumes of blended wine with no technical flaws. His arrival coincided perfectly with the new Heublein emphasis on the growth of the BV brand. Tchelistcheff was also an enologist, but his winemaking aimed at stylistically distinctive wines that showed the attributes of grape variety and vineyard site. This style was exemplified by the Georges de Latour Private Reserve, the foundation of the Beaulieu reputation, as well as the superbly Burgundian-style Pinot Noirs he had begun to make during the 1940s.

Inevitably, some of the wines that Tchelistcheff held most successful would be considered flawed from a purely scientific viewpoint, and he was dismayed by the new emphasis on wines whose cardinal virtue was being inoffensive. This enological contrast amounted to a clash of worldviews — the Old World vs. the New — and yet, the two winemakers became good friends. And the great 1970 Georges de Latour Private Reserve was among the wines that Dr. Richard Peterson and André Tchelistcheff made together.

Like Tchelistcheff three decades earlier, Peterson was dismayed by the poor state of the BV facility and winemaking equipment. André explained, "After you get to know Madame de Pins a little better, you will understand that she does not, of her own free will, put money into the winery.... She's trying to take money out of the winery, not put it in."

André never forgot that he was the last to find out about the Sullivans' decision to sell Beaulieu. But he tried to be optimistic, and persisted in trying to convince himself that new ownership meant new capital, and a glorious new age for BV. He was naturally inclined to take pleasure in life despite hardships, of which he had seen more than his share. One thing that took his mind off petty annoyances was gardening. Every day when he came home he spent the first half hour or so meditatively watering his garden. And he discovered rather late in life that he loved driving — fast driving. In 1971, at the age of seventy, André bought his first "fun" car, a chrome-yellow 240-z. Later that year he took a curve a little too fast and hit a rock, rolling the car but walking away unscathed. The car was fixed; over the next two decades André put some 240,000 miles on it — and wrecked it two more times. (The last accident, in 1990, was serious; André rolled the car on the Silverado Trail not far from the house on Stone Crest, and went to the hospital with broken ribs and multiple lacerations. The next day, his wife Dorothy sold the car.)

LEGH KNOWLES
FIGHTS FOR TRADITION

*I*nglenook was supposed to be Heublein's main wine brand. Yet Beaulieu Vineyard wines became so renowned that Heublein placed ads in magazines stating, "Our only competitor...is us." The story behind the scenes was that Heublein was running Inglenook into the ground, neglecting the top-end wines to concentrate on marketing a range of mediocre wines called Navalle. Legh Knowles felt that the integrity of Beaulieu was threatened by the attitude in Hartford. There was a lot of pressure to produce huge quantities of jug-quality wine and market it under the BV label. Knowles and Tchelistcheff had seen what that policy was doing to Inglenook, and were horrified by the

thought of what a BV equivalent of the ill-fated Navalle brand would do to the priceless de Latour reputation.

They made a formidable team that was up to the task of fending off most attempts at predation. When one bright Heublein executive suggested that all the Cabernet acreage should be replaced with Gamay because Gamay's bigger crop would produce more wine and, therefore, more money — indisputable logic from a corporate viewpoint — Knowles and Tchelistcheff were able to laugh him down. But the very fact that such an idea could be seriously entertained in Hartford was worrisome. Those were anxious times in Rutherford.

Over and over, Knowles tried to explain that a great wine is driven by vineyards and that puts a natural limit on volume. "They would say to me, 'Legh, how much do you make on Private Reserve?' I'd give them a figure, and they'd say, 'Boy, that's a lot of money. If we could make ten times as much product, we'd make ten times as much money.'" Legh tried repeatedly to make them understand why that was impossible. He introduced the mid-range line of Beau Tour wines, which sold huge quantities, based on high quality and the reputation of Private Reserve, but they weren't satisfied. They wanted more Private Reserve. He told them, "You can't sell eleven million Oldsmobiles and also eleven million Mercedes Benz."

Knowles was a battler. He decided to hang in there and do what he could for Beaulieu. It wasn't an easy ride. One day over lunch at the Brown Derby in Los Angeles, a colleague said, "You know, Legh, your days are numbered, because you don't think like they do." He knew it was true, but he meant to stick it out. And he did — in 1983 he became chairman of BV.

The competition inflicted casualties on the home team. One was Legh Knowles's brandy. He and André had established a fine-brandy program in which spirits distilled from premium wine grapes were aged in French oak barrels on the model of Cognac. At the time there was no program like it in California (Christian Brothers' vaunted brandy, though excellent, was not in the premium class, and the Rémy Martin–Schramsberg project was still years in the future), and Knowles believed that BV's Cognac-quality brandy would be the jewel in its crown.

The brandy had been aging for nearly five years — longer than Cognac's minimum requirement for VSOP — and was almost ready for bottling, when Knowles got a call from Hartford. A Heublein executive informed him that the brandy had been appropriated for another program. Incredulous, Legh asked how it would be packaged.

"Brandy Alexanders," was the reply. After five years of mellowing in casks, BV's entire VSOP program had been flushed into Heublein's line of canned cocktails.

Enraged by what was clearly a personal assault from corporate headquarters, Knowles briefly considered throwing in the towel. After a few minutes, however, it began to seem funny, a perfect illustration of what he was up against in the blind corporate mentality. He began telling the story at dinner parties, timing it for the moment after dinner when Cognac made its appearance.

Throughout the 70s, Legh Knowles's gravelly, avuncular voice became familiar to radio listeners. He seemed to be talking to you, the listener, as if resuming an ongoing conversation. "This is Legh Knowles, president of

Beaulieu Vineyard," he'd say, and people would smile and nod. "You know, here at BV…" Legh would begin, and listeners paid attention — and bought Beaulieu wines. André Tchelistcheff also cut a radio spot, and his mellifluous Russian accent seduced a new generation of BV consumers while making André California's first media-star winemaker.

Meanwhile, Heublein began conducting fine wine auctions accompanied by high-profile tastings, which considerably elevated the reputation of California wines, and Beaulieu in particular. The auctions began in Chicago in 1969 and moved to San Francisco in 1971. The big attractions were premier cru Bordeaux (in 1972 a bottle of Château Lafite, 1846 fetched $5,000), but older bottles from the Beaulieu and Inglenook cellars also attracted attention. Parcels of old vintages, such as the 1936 and 1951 Private Reserve Cabernets and the 1946 Pinot Noir routinely fetched high prices. BV's reputation as a benchmark producer of California wines was further solidified because of Heublein's wine auctions, self-serving as they may have seemed at the time. (Indeed, the magic of the BV name attached to a venerable vintage is still alive today. A twelve-bottle case of 1951 Private Reserve sold for $24,000 at a New York City auction in early 2000.)

THE MAESTRO'S
EXPANDING INFLUENCE

After a few years of Heublein ownership, André's frustration became unbearable. He had been optimistic about the corporation's commitment to improving quality; "but then, you know, time goes on, and you learn far more about corporate business," he told an interviewer in 1979. "Corporations are entirely different than private companies, and I started to gradually think we are not going to be successful in resisting any temptation in jeopardizing this quality. It's time for me to go out."

André decided to retire. Beaulieu and Heublein countered by offering him a consulting agreement with a fee that was handsome for the time. André said it suited him, and initially accepted "strings" in the contract stipulating that his name and reputation not be used in connection with another company's wines.

Then he wavered. In passionate conversations with Legh Knowles,

André deplored the direction Beaulieu seemed to be taking. He had no problem with being progressive, he said, but in his opinion Dick Peterson was not the right winemaker for BV. He felt that Peterson was inclined to make quick decisions and move too fast in changing production methods. This lack of good judgment, in his opinion, was aggravated by the fact that Peterson had little experience in producing the kind of fine wines that had earned BV its reputation. Finally, he suggested that Peterson's expertise in chemical engineering and quality control would make him more valuable in one of Heublein's large European operations.

André urged that BV hire Myron Nightingale, the Beringer Vineyards winemaker. He told Knowles that Nightingale was one of the best California winemakers and was unhappy with his job at Beringer. He also suggested making Tom Selfridge, who had been hired upon graduation from UC Davis the previous fall with high recommendations from Dr. Maynard Amerine, the backup winemaker.

In the end, André Tchelistcheff turned down the consulting contract, saying that after deep consideration he had decided to "cut with a knife" his relations with BV and Heublein. The activities mentioned in the contract, he said, would not place him in the role of a builder, but rather "a watch dog, maintenance man, and a general promoter."

André retired on April 1, 1973, at the age of seventy-two. "There is no point in attempting any further negotiations," he told Knowles. But retirement, to André, had nothing to do with ceasing work. Like Georges de Latour, who worked hard until his death at eighty-four, André continued to do what he loved. On April 2 he began consulting for Simi Winery. Retirement, in his case, was just a formality — he continued to live winemaking, day and night. Within a short time he was consulting for wineries in three states: Washington (Ste. Michelle), Oregon (Erath and Wynquist), and California (Simi, Buena Vista, Stag's Leap Wine Cellars, Hoffman Mountain Ranch, Firestone, Jordan). "I thought the challenges, new, individual aspects and efforts in entirely different ecological regions of California, Washington, and Oregon would give me far more constructive energy to end out my professional career," he explained.

He was particularly intrigued to be working with Simi winemaker Mary Ann Graf, California's first prominent female winemaker (now a

consulting enologist and proprietor of a commercial laboratory in Healdsburg). "Of course, I have younger people than Mary Ann Graf in the new
projects I'm starting," he said at the time, "but she is a challenge to me because I had been acquainted with working for women superiors, such as
Madame de Latour and Madame la Marquise de Pins at Beaulieu, but I had
never been acquainted with the idea that someday in my life I would work
parallel in a team of plowing horses with a young lady on the side of me."

A NEW GUARD TAKES OVER

*D*ick Peterson persevered through the summer, but shortly before the
1973 harvest he left Beaulieu as well. Ostensibly the attraction was an opportunity to become the founding winemaker at The Monterey Vineyard in the
Salinas Valley, but it was no secret that he'd been unhappy at BV.

"Heublein is basically a sales organization," he said later, "and I had
trouble at first making some of them understand what true quality in wine really is." He recalled a conversation with a Heublein executive just after the
takeover. The Hartford man asked Peterson why he used Chenin Blanc in BV
Champagne. "Because we don't have any excess Chardonnay," replied
Peterson.

"Oh, no, that's not what I mean," laughed the exec. "Don't you realize Thompson Seedless is only $50 a ton and you're paying $900 a ton for Chardonnay?"

"I said, 'If you think you can get me to use any Thompson Seedless in any Beaulieu Vineyard wine, we'd better just talk about something else,'" recalled Peterson. "He looked at me and kind of shook his head and said, 'Dick, you'll never make a million dollars.'"

Not everyone complained, however. Cellar manager Theo Rosenbrand, in charge of winemaking operations, found that things were easier under Heublein ownership than they had been with the family. "To me," he recalled, "the biggest change was that under the de Pins family, if I needed twenty cents I had to put in a request and fight for the money. With Heublein, if you could convince someone that you needed the money, they gave it to you. So the old redwood fermentors got canned and we got stainless steel tanks with cooling." While Inglenook suffocated under the FTC's antitrust suit, BV thrived, thanks to the profitability of Heublein's spirits business. The new influx of capital for improvements made it easier for Theo to turn down Dick Peterson's subsequent offer of the cellar manager's job at The Monterey Vineyard.

The BV cellar sustained another blow in 1978. When the Sterling Vineyards star winemaker, Ric Forman, left to start a new winery with former Sterling partner Peter Newton, Sterling management called Theo Rosenbrand and made a handsome offer that included not just money but an opportunity to study winemaking formally at the University of California at Davis. "I knew every tank and barrel in the BV cellar," recalls Theo. "Hell, I had been inside every tank. But I couldn't refuse what Sterling offered." Theo Rosenbrand left Beaulieu in time to make the 1978 wines at Sterling (where he remained until 1986). Tom Selfridge, the bright young UC Davis graduate, took over the BV cellar.

Heublein appointed Dennis Fife vice president of BV in 1979, assisting Legh Knowles primarily with the marketing issues. Fife and Legh Knowles got along famously. "He was the best salesman I ever met," says Fife. "I got to see him in action a lot, and he was amazing. He came up playing trumpet in a touring band, and his school was that you practice, practice, practice. He did the same thing with public speaking, practicing every speech or presentation over and over. And I was usually the guy he practiced on." However, Fife notes that not even Knowles's tremendous charm and photographic memory could help him in the world of corporate politics. "The only thing he never figured out," says Fife, "was how to communicate with Heublein."

In 1982 a new face appeared at Beaulieu. Joel Aiken was a young winemaker just out of UC Davis. He had done his graduate work in oak aging, which was also a specialty of André's. Although a junior member of the winemaking staff, Joel had something about him that was quintessentially BV. His education, temperament, and classical viewpoint were similar to Tchelistcheff's. Perhaps more important, he immediately felt at home in the Beaulieu vineyards and cellar, as if he were somehow meant to continue the Georges de Latour legacy. Fortunately, Joel Aiken also had the knack of communicating effectively with Heublein.

Four decades earlier, Georges de Latour had journeyed to Paris in search of an enologist to fine-tune Beaulieu wine production. André Tchelistcheff had found a great wine estate that had veered slightly off course as it entered maturity, and he had been able to focus and consolidate BV's strengths in a way that allowed BV to become the great international estate envisioned by its founders. Now, a young Californian emerged in the same capacity at another critical juncture in BV history.

MAINTAINING A
LUSTROUS REPUTATION

For all the luster of the reputation that made BV so attractive to a beverage-marketing corporation, the essence of that reputation was in jeopardy. The wines of Beaulieu had benefited for eighty years from consistency in the vineyards and cellars; many employees began working at BV in their youth and spent their entire working lives on the de Latour payroll. The BV family's persistent sensibilities in every phase of wine production, from vine pruning through bottling, also contributed to the distinctive quality of Beaulieu wines. The turmoil following the conversion from family to corporate ownership inevitably compromised that consistency and threatened that distinction.

Thus it was not an easy time for a young winemaker to debut at a

high-profile winery. The 1980s were difficult for California winemakers, not only due to continued unsettled weather (reflecting a period of particularly turbulent oceanic and atmospheric conditions) but also because California winemaking was undergoing a rapid and dynamic evolutionary phase. Yet despite all that, the Private Reserves from those years were generally among the Napa Valley's outstanding wines. One had to credit a strong team effort, as well as Joel Aiken's increasing influence on winemaking practices at BV.

He became head winemaker in 1985, just in time to make the most of the superb '85, '86, and '87 vintages, and to make Georges de Latour Private Reserve one of the few stellar Napa Valley Cabernets from the difficult '89 growing season. Joel was also one of the primary influences in the brief but influential return of André Tchelistcheff as an in-house consultant in 1991. It was hoped that his presence would inspire the young winemaking staff. It did — sometimes in unexpected ways.

One day Joel was walking through the cellar with André, who asked his young protégé how much of the Cabernet was being aged in French oak. "None," replied Joel in surprise. "We only use American oak, because that's what you used."

"But I've changed," said André. "Why haven't you?"

Joel felt as if the cellar were suddenly flooded with sunshine. He had been hoping to make some changes in the Cabernet barrel aging program, but the exclusive use of American oak had become sacrosanct. Once André made it clear that the main reason for his reliance on American oak all those years had been a matter of circumstance rather than choice, he and Joel were able to convince corporate management to spend the huge sum required to begin phasing in French oak barrels. Once again, André was instrumental in taking Beaulieu winemaking to a new level.

Unfortunately, André was still uncomfortable in the larger, corporate-owned BV. He was given a large office and felt the tremendous respect every-

one felt toward him. His old affectionate nickname, Maestro, was burnished to a high sheen on the lips of young winemakers who recognized him as a living legend, and Joel Aiken subsequently produced a Carneros Pinot Noir called "Maestro" in tribute to his mentor. And yet, André didn't feel as though he belonged. After the first day, he went home and told Dorothy, "I made a mistake." Before long, however, he rallied. Despite his early misgivings, André had to respond to the awestruck respect that greeted his return. Inspired by the young winemakers' eagerness to learn everything the master could teach them, he rediscovered his own youthful commitment to Beaulieu and within a short time was spending more time in the cellars with Joel Aiken and his colleagues than his contract required.

He was known for using colorful images to describe wine. Rob Davis (winemaker at Jordan Vineyard in Alexander Valley and one of André's consulting protégés) recalls him tasting a Cabernet and saying, "It reminds me of the breast of a young woman in a fur coat." He frequently brought up childhood memories, too. During an evening at the Clift Hotel in San Francisco that featured a blind tasting of Champagnes, he sniffed one glass and said, "Laurent Perrier." He always recognized that wine, he said, because that's what his parents had served at parties in Russia. André and his sister, Anne, used to polish off the Champagne left in glasses delivered back to the kitchen. The flavor of Laurent Perrier was emblazoned in his memory, he told the crowd, and it always reminded him of Mother Russia.

Even at the age of ninety, his wits and palate were sharp, as he demonstrated by personally blending a Napa Valley "unity lot" from 105 wines donated by Napa Valley vintners to the Napa Valley Wine Auction. His character and attitude toward life, forged in the Russian Revolution, tempered in prewar France, and polished in the once and future Napa Valley, is summed up well by an offhand quote in a 1991 newspaper profile: "Money is the dust of life. I don't have a wine cellar. I don't have nothing. I only have my head."

Like Georges de Latour, André Tchelistcheff was finally halted by cancer in the midst of his most exciting work. Devoted to wine right to the end, he had particular trouble letting go of his pet Pinot Noir project. Just before he died, in 1994, he exclaimed, "We still don't know what kind of rootstock is right for Carneros!"

*O*ne thing everyone knew by that time was what kind of rootstock was wrong, not only for Carneros but also for all of California. In the late 1980s the state's viticultural history had cycled back to its condition a century earlier, when phylloxera made its first deadly entrance. The devastation that Georges de Latour had witnessed on his business circuits through North Coast vineyards was being revisited.

Indeed, it was the wrong rootstock, AxR-1, which had opened the door to this new infestation. UC Davis and commercial nurseries had strongly recommended AxR-1 for decades, until it became the most prevalent rootstock in the state. It was an excellent rootstock aside from one fatal flaw: one of its parents was *Vitis vinifera*. That meant it wasn't completely resistant to phylloxera, and the voracious pest (which had never actually gone away) began to feast once more. By the mid-90s nearly seventy-five percent of Napa Valley vineyards would have to be replanted with truly resistant rootstocks, at a staggering cost — not just in dollars, but in the destruction of an entire generation of vines just as they entered maturity.

André Tchelistcheff was among the first in the wine community to see the light within the gathering darkness. Like Georges de Latour nearly a century earlier, he understood that beyond the short-term devastation was golden opportunity — in this case, a chance to reassess the vineyards and to upgrade them with new rootstocks, clones, and trellising systems. Specifically, his long-held dream of making great Pinot Noir in the Carneros district would be within reach.

In Joel Aiken, the Heublein managers had a winemaster it could communicate with, and who in turn was able to demonstrate to them the ultimate business sense of spending whatever was necessary to maintain Beaulieu's incomparable reputation. Heublein faced the phylloxera challenge squarely, pumping money into the winery's replanting program while continuing to upgrade equipment in the winery. Increasingly, Aiken and his team pushed for more freedom to explore better clones, trellising systems and improved cultivation techniques. Some of his innovations involved judicious steps backward to re-establish traditional methods that had been lost in the rush to embrace new technologies. In 1984 he reintroduced a few old-style

JOEL AIKEN, DIRECTOR
OF WINEMAKING AT BV

redwood fermentation tanks with open tops that allowed punching down the "cap" of skins by hand. The resulting improvement in the concentration and color of the wines (first Pinot Noir, later Cabernet) was so impressive that he won funding for an array of small, open-top stainless steel tanks with a pneumatic punch-down piston above each tank. He also instituted the costly and labor-intensive process of fermenting Chardonnay in French oak barrels. Joel's argument was always the same: that spending whatever it took to get it right the first time would not only save money later but allow for more profitable and prestigious wines in the future as well.

Legh Knowles had made much the same case in 1980 when he won funding for BV's Cabernet clonal experiments in conjunction with UC Davis. The fourteen-year study (continued from 1987–1994 by BV viticulturist Michael Salacci, now winemaker at Stag's Leap Wine Cellars) was the most detailed and extensive clonal assessment ever undertaken in California, and it benefited the entire wine industry. The most important result for BV was the emergence of two distinguished clones that yield consistently fine Cabernet Sauvignon wines in Rutherford. Clones 4 and 6 became the mainstays of the newly replanted Beaulieu vineyards in Rutherford.

By 1993 Joel Aiken was in firm and complete control of the winegrowing at BV, and seeing the fruits of his initial changes made a few years before coming to fruition with critical praise and increased sales. Ever since André Tchelistcheff's brief but powerful reappearance in the BV cellars, Aiken had worn the mantle of Beaulieu winemaster with increasing confidence and authority. One salient result was that French oak played an increasingly important role in red wine aging, bringing finesse and subtlety to the regally intense Cabernets from the newly fine-tuned Private Reserve vineyards in Rutherford.

Another frontier was BV's first Zinfandel and Sangiovese, which appeared with the 1994 vintage. Georges de Latour never produced a Zinfandel — after all, it wasn't French — and would have ignored Sangiovese, too, if there had been any in Napa Valley early in the twentieth century (it only appeared in the late 80s). But when Heublein purchased the Christian Brothers

Brand in 1989 it acquired several mature Zinfandel vineyards in St. Helena and Calistoga, and Aiken strongly urged the Executive Group to consider producing California's signature varietal under the BV label. The result was a new and exciting BV varietal program known as Signet, which has now grown to include Rhône-style wines like Syrah, Viognier, and Grenache.

Aiken continued to receive strong support as the new Coastal tier of lower-priced regional wines he masterminded came into the market, replacing the dated Beau Tour program. The Coastal bottlings, primarily from vineyards in California's Central Coast region, have gained strong momentum in the popular market. Like the Beau Tour bottlings of a previous era, these delicious and affordable wines complement the more serious and expensive vineyard-driven wines from BV's Napa Valley holdings.

Through shifts in fortune and adverse circumstances, against the hard and sometimes conflicting realities of agriculture and business, the de Latour legacy has been nurtured by dedicated, capable, often brilliant people who share the founders' vision of Beaulieu. At the turn of one century, Georges and Fernande de Latour fell in love with a place in the sun along an unpaved Napa Valley road. Through the hundred years leading to the new millennium, the Beaulieu vineyards and winery have produced wines that speak eloquently of the Napa Valley sun and the Rutherford dust, and the passion of the Beaulieu Vineyard family.

Bottled History

*N*o California winery (nor, for that matter, *any* New World winery) can offer a bottled record to match the sixty-four vintages of Beaulieu Vineyard Georges de Latour Private Reserve Cabernet Sauvignon, from 1936–2000 (no Private Reserve was bottled in 1937). Georges de Latour Private Reserve was California's first prestige bottling, and it became a true benchmark for California wine, especially Napa Valley Cabernet Sauvignon.

Appropriately, it debuted after Georges de Latour had already been growing grapes and making wine for more than three decades. The first Beaulieu Vineyard wines were made in the John Thomann winery (which was later purchased by Sutter Home). In 1909, wine was made in the Henry Harris winery, on the Silverado Trail east of Rutherford. Veteran winemaker Henry Stice directed Joseph Ponti and the BV crew. The following year wine was again made in the Henry Harris winery by Joseph Ponti and crew with Henry Stice advising.

In 1911, wine was made at Beaulieu for the first time in any quantity. The old Thompson stable had already been converted to a storage and bottling facility, and was now modified and reinforced for full-scale wine production. It produced five vintages. Meanwhile, a new winery was built on the property and used for the first time in the 1916 crush; this building served as the Beaulieu winery for seven vintages.

The de Latours purchased the Fred Ewer winery, across the county road from the Beaulieu estate, in 1923. That old stone building was originally the Ewer & Atkinson Winery, built in the 1880s by Fred's father, former California Senator Seneca Ewer. It remains the core of the present BV winery. The facility was expanded continually through 1942. Much of it was destroyed in a large fire in the fall of 1947, but it was subsequently rebuilt and expanded further.

The first Georges de Latour Private Reserve was 1936. That wine was still in barrel when André Tchelistcheff arrived at BV in 1938, so he was involved in every vintage of Private Reserve through the 1972 vintage, and also in 1991–1994 as a consultant.

New French oak barrels were used for the first few vintages, but World War II interfered with shipments and the only alternative was domestically produced American oak barrels from the whisky cooperages in Kentucky. André made a virtue out of necessity, washing the barrels out with soda ash and rinsing with citric acid, then seasoning them with other wines for two years or more before using them to age Private Reserve. That tamed the "whisky lactone" character of the American oak, so that the time in wood served to round and smooth the wine without imparting strong flavor. The wine was aged entirely in American oak until 1989, when Joel Aiken acted on André's suggestion to reintroduce French oak. At that time Joel also increased the percentage of new barrels; this was made possible by a new generation of American oak barrels coopered in the French manner from hand-

split, air-dried staves that are bent and toasted over an open oak-chip fire, all of which makes for a more subtle and integrated effect on the wine. There is no precise oak "recipe." However, Private Reserve cuvées from the 90s on have typically been aged half in American oak barrels and half in French, with the percentage of new oak barrels ranging between fifty and seventy-five percent (only '95 was one hundred percent new). Also, the secondary fermentation (malolactic) now takes place in barrels rather than tanks.

With only two exceptions, the Georges de Latour Private Reserve has always been one hundred percent Cabernet Sauvignon. In 1990 and 1991 Joel Aiken blended in small amounts of Merlot, but subsequently returned to Cabernet alone. The wine was initially produced from BV#1, the estate vineyard in Rutherford. Over time, fruit from BV#2, located two miles south, was incorporated; in the 1940s, while

BV#1 was being replanted, up to two-thirds of the Private Reserve came from BV#2. The Cabernet vines at BV#2 were propagated from the vines at BV#1. The BV selection of Cabernet originally came from the famous Sullivan Nursery outside Paris. The nursery no longer exists; a recent attempt to trace the selection farther back to a specific part of Bordeaux was unsuccessful.

The BV vineyards have been completely replanted twice since World War II, in the 1960s and 90s. The first time, propagation material was rigorously selected from existing vines that showed the least signs of the leaf-roll virus which was rampant in previous plantings to the detriment of fruit maturity. In 1980 a long-term micro-vinification program was initiated to evaluate more than a dozen Cabernet clones. Two of them, UCD-4 and UCD-6, were selected when the phylloxera infestation made it necessary to replant BV#1 and BV#2 in the 1990s.

The second major replanting coincided with decisive changes in the BV cellar initiated by winemaker Joel Aiken. "This was a time of huge changes in our philosophy. There was no formula — we decided to get rid of all the old recipes and do what we thought was best." One of the things they thought was best was picking the grapes more ripe, which mean less acidulation. They also concentrated on the new Cabernet clones they'd planted, while incorporating an unprecedented ratio of French oak.

ROBERT MASYCZEK,
BV WINEMAKER

at right:
SHOVELING OUT THE
POMACE FROM AN
OPEN-TOP REDWOOD
WINE FERMENTOR
AFTER THE WINE HAS
BEEN DRAINED OFF
FOR PRESSING

*A*ll but four of the Georges de Latour Private Reserves through 1998 were tasted in London on July 20, 1999 (none was made in '37; the '38, '40, and '44 were unobtainable). Most of the early vintages came from Dagmar and Walter Sullivan's personal cellar; others came from the BV cellar or were purchased from private collectors. The tasting was held at Vinopolis. Tasters included: Joel Aiken, Jeffrey Stambor, Bob Masyczek (Beaulieu Vineyard winemakers); Joel Butler (Master of Wine, Beaulieu Vineyard); Priscilla Felton (Beaulieu Vineyard marketing); Michael Broadbent (Christie's); John Salvi (Master of Wine, Bordeaux); Michael Schuster (journalist, London); Stephen Spurrier (consultant, London); Oz Clarke (journalist, London); Hugh Johnson (writer, London); Stephen Brook (writer, London); Jim Suckling (senior editor, *Wine Spectator*); Robert Joseph (editor, *Wine*); Charles Olken (editor/writer, San Francisco); and the author. The wines were not ranked or numerically rated. These descriptions incorporate the author's notes on the wines and observations from the intensive discussions between flights; some of the more interesting comments are followed by the taster's initials.

1936 The 1936 growing season began with a bitter frost that drastically reduced the crop. Subsequent weather was fine, however, and the grapes ripened fully and evenly through a moderate summer and fall. The bottle tasted in July, 1999 in London was only filled partway up the shoulder; as expected, the wine was disappointing.

1938 Some meteorologists have suggested that the vintages of the late 30s reflected El Niño-like conditions, although the phenomenon itself wasn't fully understood until the 1990s. In any case, the 1937 growing season was cool and wet, and no Private Reserve was produced. Very little was produced in 1938, another difficult vintage; it is believed that most of the potential Private Reserve wine that year was blended into the Burgundy and Claret.

1939 A drier, warmer season yielded a fine Private Reserve that was still impressive in 1999, with a chocolatey undertone.

1940 The wettest year on record (until El Niño set new records in the 80s). A mild growing season produced a good, if light, wine that was still showing well in the early 90s.

1941 Long considered one of the Napa Valley's best vintages. The 1941 Private Reserve was still big, round, and elegant in '99, with a wonderful Cabernet sweetness on the palate.

1942 Unsettled spring weather foreshortened the growing season, producing a wine that was somewhat lighter than the '41 although still very fine. In '99 it was remarkably fresh at the heart of its well-aged Cabernet palate, and richly textured.

ANDRÉ TCHELISTCHEFF TASTING THE 1936 AND 1986
BV CABERNET PRIVATE RESERVES, C.1990

1943 More unsettled weather produced another fairly light Private Reserve, which in '99 had a high-toned perfume with a note of dry wood shavings, and a youthful grip. "If you close your eyes you could be sipping a five-year-old Madeira."(MB) "A cross between a really good Tawny Port and Australian Shiraz. The first one really to show some signs of jumping around." (OC)

1944 A textbook growing season — short, uniform flowering and set followed by a moderate growing season — yielded a classic Private Reserve, but not much of it, and some was lost in the winery fire of 1947. The '44 was still a beautiful wine in the early 90s, but is now extremely rare.

1945 The 1945 vintage was similar to '44, so perhaps the '45 Private Reserve gives some notion of what the previous vintage would be like now. In the '99 retrospective it showed a wonderful luxuriant silkiness and fine weight on the palate, good balance, and a smooth transfer of weight through the palate into a lingering finish.

1946 A frost-free spring and a long, warm season produced perfectly ripe fruit — and a brilliant garnet-brick Private Reserve with a spicy-earthy nose, plump and silky palate, and that sharp whiff of clean dirt that shows up increasingly as we move into the vintages that are in their prime. "Elegant, with bright fruit." (JA) "It's elegant, gracious, absolutely beautiful." (JSa) (8,095 CASES PRODUCED)

1947 A warm spring opened this fateful year in which a fire destroyed two buildings and some 800,000 gallons of wine. An early bud break was followed by tranquil weather ideal for flowering and fruit set. Steady warmth ripened the moderate crop to perfection and yielded a notable Private Reserve. It's a medium-weight wine, a little lean on the palate but rich in the finish, pointed up by a whiff of clean earth. "I found some leanness in the finish, possibly from higher acidity." (JSt) "A certain austerity that I found quite beautiful." (JSa) "We're starting to see a dustiness. Is that the barrels, or the so-called Rutherford dust? It's almost like very fine coal dust coming through." (OC) "I think it's actually the fruit. I think today as we pick riper and riper we see less of what my interpretation of Rutherford dust would be. We see more of the cherry fruit." (JA)

1948 Rains during the harvest kept much of the unusually large crop from ripening. For once, the Rutherford Cabernet exceeded the Private Reserve, which was past reasonable assessment by '99. The Rutherford bottling was also poured, however, and although light was still bright and firm. "It's still showing fairly well after fifty years, for what was probably a seventy-five cent wine." (JA) (3,000 CASES PRODUCED)

1949 The poor '48 vintage was followed by a very cold, wet winter and spring. The crop was small and uneven, the season on the cool side. The 1949 Private Reserve was BV's only Cabernet that year. In '99 it still had youthful color, with a berryish nose and tart acidity. (9,153 CASES PRODUCED)

1950 A severe May frost in the spring reduced the crop substantially, as in 1936. Like the first Private Reserve, the '50 was a beautifully perfumed and concentrated wine, still offering deep flavor and firm acidity in '99, although beginning to fade.

1951 Fine spring weather and a moderate summer produced a modest crop of uniformly ripe grapes in 1951. The '51 Private Reserve is still considered one of the finest California wines. In '99 it was a deep, dark, beauty with fresh garnet-brick hue, an expansive ripe nose with an upper register of black cherry and berries, then gentle and silky on the palate with fine-grained texture. (ABOUT 3,500 CASES PRODUCED)

1952 Another late frost spring set up a small crop that ripened well through a dry, warm summer. The '52 is another big, powerful Private Reserve — yet a little finer and more elegant than the '51.

1953 Another April frost, not so fortuitous this time. The crop was minuscule and ripened unevenly. Still, the '53 Private Reserve was acclaimed, what little there was of it. In '99 it had good color and clarity, with an effusive, earthy nose and a touch of mint, and bright acidity. "I find it a little funky, Burgundian." (JA) "The European palate likes a bit of funk." (MS) "Very much alive, absolutely." (SS)

1954 The 1954 growing season was so favorable, and the crop so large, that all the fruit from BV#1 was sold, and the Private Reserve made from BV#2. The wine now shows classic mature Cabernet character with a cedary overtone.

1955 As usual, Mother Nature turned around and delivered unsettled spring weather after the tranquil preceding spring. Late frost reduced the crop, and it rained through the harvest. The wine was on the lighter side but remarkably fresh and vital in '99.

1956 A wet, mild winter and spring heralded this marvelous vintage. The '56 Private Reserve was in good form for the London tasting — youthful color, a ripe, focused nose leading to more of the same on the palate with nice weight and texture through a radiant Rutherford Cabernet finish.

1957 A very large crop and an uneven summer produced a rather diffuse wine that was just fading in '99.

1958 The 1958 growing season was exceptional, and so was the '58 Private Reserve. Hailed in its youth, it was praised in 1999 as well for its deep, brilliant color, the magnificent scale and complexity of its Rutherford Cabernet fruit, its luscious mid-palate, and clear note of Rutherford dust. (5,984 CASES PRODUCED)

1959 The growing season was similar to the previous year, and the '59 Private Reserve echoes the '58, if on a slightly smaller scale. Several tasters compared this pair with the beauties from '51 and '52. (5,227 CASES PRODUCED)

1960 Through the 1960s the Beaulieu vineyards were replanted. The '60 Private Reserve was the last wine made from Georges de Latour's original plantings. The growing season was moderate and the wine is on the lighter side, but it still made a vibrant impression with firm, supple tannins and intense fruit through the palate. "Vigorous, powerful, ripe." (OC) "I thought it was quite fine, but fading a little, beginning to dry out." (MS) (8,760 CASES PRODUCED)

1961 A devastating frost during the spring of '61 motivated Beaulieu's investment in a proactive frost protection program. The small crop ripened well, although rain during harvest delayed ripening. The '61 is light and on the lean side, with flavors in the berryish range of Cabernet. (3,930 CASES PRODUCED)

1962 The summer was cool and humid, with high mildew risk that prompted a rather early harvest while the grapes were firm and acid still high. In '99 the 1962 Private Reserve was pale and tasted a little like Tawny Port. "I think it's a beautiful example of the sweetness of death." (JS) "Demerara sugar." (OC) (5,672 CASES PRODUCED)

1963 A heat wave followed by heavy rain marked the harvest of '63, producing a light Private Reserve that was still fresh and lively in the mid-80s but was tart and fruitless in '99. "A horrible vintage, harvested at a high of 19.2 brix; some of the wine received brandy." (JA) (4,332 CASES PRODUCED)

1964 Even heat without spikes allowed the modest crop (reduced slightly by a nip of spring frost) to ripen well. The 1964 Private Reserve was full-bodied and vibrant for twenty years, but was noticeably drying by '99 although still absolutely Rutherford in the nose. "This was considered great at ten years old, and everybody thought it would age well, but it hasn't." (JA) "The high acidity gives it a slightly bony character." (MS) (12,145 CASES PRODUCED)

1965 The mercury hit 111 degrees F. in Rutherford during the summer of 1965, a notorious brush-fire season. Although drying and on the brown side of brick in '99, the '65 Private Reserve still showed some of its bold, ripe flavors, suppleness, and firm acidity. (7,715 CASES PRODUCED)

1966 A fine spring and warm summer ripened the fairly small crop to perfection. The '66 still has rosy cheeks and a lively nose with a dry cedar note; there's a charming red-fruit sweetness on the palate. An elegant wine with beautiful purity of fruit and velvety texture. (7,659 CASES PRODUCED)

1967 The growing season was cool, producing a classic Private Reserve that balanced the perfume and flavors of ripe Rutherford Cabernet with bright acidity and fine tannin. In London the '67 still showed those qualities in a beautifully evolved form. "It's never been a compromise, it's always been right there." (JB) "Elegant, controlled, a little austere — right bank or left bank? Right on the nose, left on the palate." (JS) (12,396 CASES PRODUCED)

1968 Warm spring, warm summer, warm autumn — the warmth (without extreme heat) of the 1968 season is still apparent in the '68 Private Reserve. Deep, clear garnet, rich on entry and right through the palate, with slightly chewy tannin and radiant length. Similar to the '67 in character, but more heroically proportioned. "I love the power because there's so much complexity to go with it. A few years ago I thought it was going over the hill, but since then it's getting better and better." (JB) (14,260 CASES PRODUCED)

1969 Another cool year produced a 1969 Private Reserve that was ripe yet focused and a little austere in youth. By '99 it had bloomed to full maturity, a magnificent mature Cabernet with elegance, complexity, and length. (11,830 CASES PRODUCED)

1970 The growing season is famous for the longest frost on record (twenty-eight straight nights) followed by spring heat that caused shatter. The crop was reduced to about two tons per acre, one of the lowest crops on record. The '70 Private Reserve has long been revered for its combination of elegance and power, for its earthy Rutherford Cabernet perfume and depth of fruit on the palate. In '99 it had very good color and a clear note of Rutherford dust in the slightly spicy nose, and was firm, round, and elegant on the palate. "A lot like the '68 but better balance." (JA) (12,750 CASES PRODUCED)

1971 A trouble-free season yielded another medium-bodied Rutherford classic; in '99 the '71 Private Reserve was bright garnet-brick, with a clear note of Rutherford, firm and gracious on the palate. "Pure, elegant, finesse." (JS) (17,000 CASES PRODUCED)

1972 A wet, cool season yielded a light-bodied Private Reserve which nonetheless had intense Rutherford Cabernet character. It has aged very well, developing a lovely high-toned perfume, plummy palate, and fine, complex finish. "Remarkable intensity for the vintage, broad on the palate, the finish isn't breaking up at all." (HJ) (12,680 CASES PRODUCED)

1973 The warm and tranquil season recalled '68 in its steady heat without spikes. The '73 Private Reserve was bold and powerful, and has aged into mature beauty with a generous Rutherford perfume scented with dried herbs, concentrated yet high-toned flavor and tannin that sort of paves the palate so the wine can drive on it. "Powerful tar character, still a very tannic wine, not subtle or elegant in any way, but it's aging well." (JA) "Racy as opposed to shrewd." (HJ) (26,000 CASES PRODUCED)

1974 With the new plantings of the previous decade maturing, their roots driving deep into the Rutherford subsoil, the wines were increasingly consistent in showing the prized Beaulieu-Rutherford character. The superb 1974 vintage yielded a classic — rich, layered, harmonious, and elegant, even in '99. "I think it deserves its reputation. Acidity gives it a lot of life and spice." (MB) A cool spring delayed bud break in 1975, but it remained cool enough to extend ripening. (29,900 CASES PRODUCED)

1975 Another fine summer yielded yet another classic Private Reserve. The '75 shows a little more herbaceousness in the nose than the '74 but with good body and concentrated mature

Cabernet flavor, although a little drying on the palate in '99. "I found it charming, I must say — pretty nose, minty, cool on the palate, didn't have all the necessary dimensions, but it did have charm." (HJ) (23,390 CASES PRODUCED)

1976 The first of two drought vintages yielded a small crop of little, thick-skinned grapes that made a deeply-colored, intense Private Reserve. The '76 was impressive in '99, its generous nose leading to a palate impression of ripe, sweet fruit with a roasted undertone and a touch of tar, and a lingering finish. "I

THE EVOLUTION OF THE PRIVATE RESERVE LABEL AND BOTTLE THROUGH SIX DECADES

fall in love with its richness, sweetness, and complexity, although the aroma is a little older than I would expect." (JA) (11,290 CASES PRODUCED)

1977 The second of the late '70s drought years was significantly cooler. Long, even ripening produced a wine that was lighter (and less tannic) than the '76, yet deeply concentrated and elegant. The '77 Private Reserve has aged well, still impressively intense and firm in '99. (22,400 CASES PRODUCED)

1978 Relief from drought came in the rainstorms of early '78, which were followed by a glorious growing season that produced concentrated Cabernet grapes. The '78 Private Reserve was still in its prime in '99, perhaps beginning to dry a bit in the finish but still complex and harmonious. (23,000 CASES PRODUCED)

LEGH KNOWLES, PAST PRESIDENT OF BV, PARTICIPATING IN A WINE TASTING

1979 Growing conditions were almost as good as '78, and the BV vineyards were harvested just before a warm October rainstorm hit the coast. The '79 Private Reserve was dark and concentrated with substantial tannin. In maturity the fruit has yielded to the tannin, but there's still a lingering Cabernet sweetness. (23,000 CASES PRODUCED)

1980 The long, cool growing season culminated in a surge of warmth that brought the grapes to high ripeness without a loss of acidity. The '80 Private Reserve still has a fresh, ripe nose with a coffee undertone and plump, sweet fruit in the mouth, almost chewy tannin. "I love the fruit, very spicy, but almost vicious acidity and teeth-gripping tannin. The nose is very good." (MB) "It leads into a decade of big, chunky wines, sort of broad-shouldered wines with brisk acidity." (SS) (22,700 CASES PRODUCED)

1981 A dry winter, timely bud break, and hot summer led to an early harvest. The fast ripening track produced fruit that was slightly less concentrated than in '80 yet with brighter acidity. The '80 Private Reserve was luscious and structured through its first decade, but has aged precipitously. "A very hot vintage. The fruit came in early and the wine was always hot. Even before it was old it was awkward." (JA) (14,900 CASES PRODUCED)

1982 Another hot summer, but not before the ground was replenished by heavy winter rains. There was more rain at harvest, but the Beaulieu Cabernet was harvested in time to yield a dark, brilliant 1982 Private Reserve with intense flavor and good structure. "Beautiful wine." (HJ) (24,100 CASES PRODUCED)

1983 The season was hot until September, when cooler temperatures delayed ripening, at some expense to concentration and definition. The '83 Private Reserve was diffuse and astringent by '99. (23,200 CASES PRODUCED)

1984 Yet another hot summer. Very ripe fruit yielded a fleshy, tannic Private Reserve that was received well in its youth but then lost fruit — and charm — as it aged. (23,350 CASES PRODUCED)

1985 Spring and early summer were dry and warm. As the crop set and began ripening, the weather cooled off and the grapes ripened fully. The '85 Private Reserve was just hitting its mark in '99, with rich fruit over firm tannin and a clear note of Rutherford dust in the finish. (19,600 CASES PRODUCED)

1986 The growing season cool and long, similar to '77. The '86 Private Reserve has a marvelous Rutherford Cabernet perfume with notes of cherry and savory herbs and a lingering, focused finish. It was not nearly mature in 1999. (9,230 CASES PRODUCED)

1987 Even, moderate heat produced a harmonious beauty with nothing in excess except perhaps the chewy tannin. In '99 the '87 Private Reserve showed a sultry, pulpy quality in the nose, within a charming, almost fey perfume of Cabernet and red roses. "This has always been a big, tannic wine but it's showing better today than I've ever seen it. It'll never be a soft, gentle wine but the tannin will soften in a couple of years. In the past it would have been a couple of years before these wines ever made it to barrel." (JA) "Pure and sweet." (HJ) (16,000 CASES PRODUCED)

1988 Unusually warm spring weather encouraged the vines to bud early, whereupon Mother Nature played a cruel trick with visitations of rain and subnormal temperatures. Flowering and fruit set were disrupted, and the season got off to a disorderly start — whereupon she delivered another reversal in the form of sustained heat which ripened the uneven crop early. The '88 Private Reserve was forward and succulent early on, and aged better than expected — in '99 it was gracious and lovely, with a nubby silk texture on the palate. (9,750 CASES PRODUCED)

1989 Few California vintages have been labeled truly bad, but 1989 is one of them. Unfortunately, that reputation is undeserved. The press made too much of heavy September rains, prematurely dismissing the entire vintage as washed out. In fact, the season had been fine until the first storm rolled in, and Beaulieu wisely waited out the rain and picked the fruit at optimum ripeness. In '99 it was a ripe, powerful wine with a little mint and eucalyptus in the nose and a rich palate impression, dense and chewy with good acidity. "That was the first year we introduced some French oak into the blend." (JA) "If we'd picked before the rain we would have had very lean, green wine." (JSt) (16,800 CASES PRODUCED)

1990 The warm spring and subsequent rain limited the fruit set. The small crop produced an unusual but delicious '90 Private Reserve. The wine had a ripe redfruit nose, very cherrylike and rich but not heavy — and, it had five percent Merlot. "The oak brings a complexing element. I think it's necessary to the varietal identity. It makes it richer in the mouth than the acidulated wines of the 80s, although not quite so rich and fat as wines from later in the 90s." (JSt) (9,825 CASES PRODUCED)

1991 Unsettled spring weather opened into a temperate summer, producing an intense '91 Private Reserve with deep concentration and high natural acidity; another rare instance of the use of small amounts of Merlot. "A very good wine indeed." (MB) "More supple and integrated than '90, the oak has bumped up the fruit but it's not obvious oak at this stage." (JA) (9,100 CASES PRODUCED)

1992 The summer began on the cool side but warmed up gradually through July and August — then cooled again in September, which delayed ripening and ultimately produced intensely flavored grapes with good natural acidity. The '92 Private Reserve has high-toned Cabernet aromas set off by toasty oak, with a fleshy richness on the palate. Its early drinkability led some to predict an early demise, but in '99 it was youthful and showing very well. (10,300 CASES PRODUCED)

1993 Another early harvest due to widely fluctuating temperatures, mostly on the hot side. Hard tannin and lots of oak marked the '93 Private Reserve, but in '99 it showed signs of beginning a sustained bloom. "It's not tight in comparison with some of the wines of the 80s." (OC) (13,300 CASES PRODUCED)

1994 April rain was followed by ideal weather in May to kick off a long, slow ripening that produced concentrated and uniformly ripe fruit. The '94 Private Reserve was deeply colored, with a spicy nose (and a touch of mint) and

ANDRÉ TCHELISTCHEFF SAMPLING WINE IN THE BV
CELLAR, C.1986

layers of fruit and tannin. Big and hard in
the first blush of youth, it had grown into
charismatic adolescence by '99. "The integra-
tion with the oak is not quite there yet but the
potential is there for a great wine." (MB)
(15,200 CASES PRODUCED)

1995 The unsettled spring followed by a hot
summer made 1995 less than perfect, which
made it an off-year in the 90s. The '95 Private
Reserve was difficult to assess in '99 because of
its youth and the almost shocking intensity of
oak in the wine. It was, in fact, the first (and
only) time Joel Aiken used one hundred percent new oak to age a Private Reserve. "It's
interchangeable with a new-style Burgundy."
(SS) "I like this style." (OC) (13,000 CASES
PRODUCED)

1996 Hail struck in the spring, an extremely rare
occurrence that was uncannily timed to reduce
the crop. The grapes then ripened quickly and
well during a hot summer, only to slow down
as the temperature cooled in early September.
The '96 Private Reserve is a broader, fatter,
fleshier wine than '95, with liberal oak seasoning, rich black fruit, softer tannin and an
apparent absence of Rutherford dust. "I hope
you do turn the oak down. It's Glorious Tech-
nicolor. I'm concerned that other regions, not
just Bordeaux, will try to make wines like
this." (MB) (13,000 CASES PRODUCED)

1997 The Centennial Vintage of Georges de Latour
Private Reserve was anomalous: a fine vintage
with a huge crop of superb quality. Nobody
can remember a crop so large that was so
good. The 1997 Private Reserve is a powerful,
succulent, finely structured beauty in its
youth. Everyone at Vinopolis in July, 1999
expressed a desire to taste it in ten years —
and twenty, and…but it may outlive all of us.
(barrel sample) (APPROXIMATELY 19,000 CASES
WILL BE PRODUCED)

Acknowledgments

"He who plants a vine becomes entangled in its branches."
— Gustave Flaubert

The author wishes to thank everyone who opened their archives, memories and hearts to provide information for this book. The definitive biographies of both Georges de Latour and André Tchelistcheff have yet to be written. New information on all aspects of the BV story continues to flow in even as we go to press, and new sources will undoubtedly be stimulated by the publication of this book. Any omissions or errors are strictly my own.

I'm particularly grateful to Dagmar de Pins Sullivan and Dorothy Tchelistcheff. Their gracious accommodation and patience made this book possible; their hospitality made it a pleasure.

Historian William F. Heintz made an important contribution through research and interviews commissioned by Legh Knowles in the early 1970s and preserved in the BV archives. Most notably, his interviews with the late Joseph Ponti and Otto Gramlow captured valuable information just before it would have been lost forever.

I especially want to thank Joel Butler and Priscilla Felton for getting me involved in the project, and Gaetano Maida for making it happen.

Rod Smith
San Francisco, California
4 July 2000

Sources

Adams, Leon. *The Wines of America.* New York: McGraw-Hill, 1978.

Aiken, Joel W. Author interview, 2000.

———. "Comparison of the Effects of Storage in French and American Oak Barrels on the Composition and Sensory Properties of Cabernet Sauvignon Wine." Master's thesis, University of California, 1983.

Aiken, Joel W. and Noble. A.C. "Comparison of the Aromas of Oak- and Glass-Aged Wines." *American Journal of Enology and Viticulture,* Vol. 35 #4.

Asher, Gerald. *On Wine.* New York: Random House, 1982.

Beckstoffer, Andrew. Author interviews, 1997–2000.

Behr, Edward. *Prohibition: Thirteen Years that Changed America.* New York: Arcade, 1996.

Benson, Robert. *Great Winemakers of California.* Santa Barbara: Capra Press, 1977.

Conaway, James. *Napa.* Boston: Houghton Mifflin, 1990.

Cuneo, Gene. Interviewed by Carole Hicke. Winegrowers of Dry Creek Valley Oral History Program, 1998.

De Latour, Georges. Personal correspondence. Beaulieu Vineyard Archive.

De Pins, Hélène. *Memoir.* Beaulieu Vineyard Archive.

Davis, Rob. Author interview, 1999.

Di Rosa, Rene. Author interview, 1999.

Elliott-Fisk, Deborah L. "Viticultural Soils of California, with Special Reference to the Napa Valley." *Journal of Wine Research* Vol. 4 #2.

Elliott-Fisk, Deborah L. and Noble, Ann C. "The Diversity of Soils and Environments in Napa Valley, California and Their Influence on Cabernet Sauvignon Wine Flavors." *Miami Geographical Society* 1996.

Fife, Dennis. Author interviews, 1998–2000.

Fisher, M.F.K. *The Story of Wine in California.* Berkeley: University of California Press, 1962.

Gladstones, John. *Viticulture and Environment.* Adelaide: Winetitles, 1992.

Gramlow, Otto P. Interviewed by William F. Heintz. Beaulieu Vineyard Archive, 1974.

Heintz, William. *California's Napa Valley.* San Francisco: Scottwall Associates, 1999.

Hobart, Alice Tisdale. *The Cup and the Sword.* New York: Bobbs-Merrill, 1942.

Hussmann, George. *Grape Culture and Wine-making in California: a practical manual for the grape-grower and wine-maker.* San Francisco: Payot-Upham, 1888.

Johnson, Hugh. *Vintage: The Story of Wine.* London: Mitchell Beazley, 1989.

Knowles, Legh. University of California Oral History Project. Bancroft Library.

Lapsley, James T. *Bottled Poetry.* Berkeley: University of California Press, 1996.

McNeill, William H. *A World History.* Oxford: Oxford University Press, 1999.

McPhee, John. *Assembling California.* New York: Farrar, Straus and Giroux, 1993.

Ministry of Agriculture, Fisheries, and Food. *Catalogue of Selected Wine Grape Varieties and Clones Cultivated in France.* Paris, 1997.

Mondavi, Robert. Author interview, 1998.

Penning-Rowsell, Edmund. *The Wines of Bordeaux.* New York: Stein and Day, 1972.

Peterson, Dr. Richard. Author interview, 1999.

Perdue, Lewis. *The Wrath of Grapes.* New York: Avon, 1999.

Ponti, Joseph J. Interviewed by William F. Heintz, 1974.

Robinson, Jancis. *Guide to Wine Grapes.* Oxford: Oxford University Press, 1998.

Rolle, Andrew. *California, A History.* Wheeling: Harlan Davidson, 1998.

Rosenbrand, Theo. Author interview, 2000.

San Francisco Voter Register File, 1888–1905. California State Library.

Selfridge, Tom. Author interviews, 1987–1999.

Service, Robert. *A History of Twentieth Century Russia.* Cambridge: Harvard University Press, 1997.

Smart, Richard. *Sunlight into Wine.* Adelaide: Winetitles, 1991.

Smith, Rod. *Terrain & Terroir, A Napa Valley Primer.* St. Helena: Napa Valley Vintners Association, 1997.

———. *Weather into Wine. A Napa Valley Vintage Primer.* St. Helena: Napa Valley Vintners Association, 1999.

Smith, Rod and Thompson, Bob. *Wine Country California.* Menlo Park: Lane Publishing Co., 1987.

Sorensen, Lorin. *Beringer.* St. Helena: Silverado Publishing Company, 1989.

Sullivan, Dagmar. Author interviews, 1999–2000.

Tchelistcheff, André. Interviewed by Ruth Teiser. University of California Oral History Project, 1979.

———. Author interviews, 1981, 1986.

Tchelistcheff, André and Graff, Richard H. "Producing and Aging Wine in Small Oak Cooperage." *Wines & Vines* May 1969.

Tchelistcheff, Dorothy. Author interviews, 1999–2000.

Thompson, Bob and Johnson, Hugh. *The California Wine Book.* New York: William Morrow, 1976.

Tonella, Louis. Author interview, 1999.

Tonella, Ray. Author interview, 1999.

University of California. *Grape Pest Management.* Davis, 1992.

Unwin, Tim. *Wine and the Vine.* London: Routledge, 1991.

Wait, Frona Eunice. *Wines and Vines of California.* Berkeley: Bancroft, 1889.

Weber, Lin. *Old Napa Valley.* St. Helena: Wine Ventures, 1998.

Wente, Ernest. Interviewed by Ruth Teiser. University of California Oral History Project, 1971.

Yonge, C.D., translator. *The Orations of Marcus Tullius Cicero.* London: G.E. Bell, 1877.

PRODUCED BY A/M Studios

MANAGING EDITOR: Gaetano Kazuo Maida
CREATIVE DIRECTION: Halleck

ART DIRECTOR: Ayelet Maida
EDITOR: D. Patrick Miller
EDITORIAL ADVISOR: James Norwood Pratt
TECHNICAL ADVISOR: Joel Butler, MW

PHOTOGRAPHY:
Andy Katz photographed at Beaulieu Vineyard properties over the course of a full year; his images are presented throughout the book without captions: front and back jacket, II–III, IV, VI–VII, VIII, X–I, 3, 6–7, 10, 12–13, 14–15, 19, 20, 22, 24–25, 32–33, 41, 44–45, 49, 52–53, 61, 62, 64–65, 69, 72–73, 76, 84–85, 87, 90–91, 93, 100, 104, 106–107, 113, 118–119, 128–129, 133, 136–137, 139, 143, 148, 155, 156, 160, 161, 162 (top)

All other photographs are courtesy the Beaulieu Vineyard archives, with individual photographers or sources identified where known:

California Historical Society: 110, 111; Scott Clemens: 170; Marvin Collins: 152; Faith Echtermeyer: 164; Allan Flood: 103, 108; Gracelyn & Burns: 140; Michael Landis: 98; Fred Lyon: 2, 28, 56, 95, 116, 122, 125; Gabriel Moulin Studios: 39, 42, 55, 75, 82, 127 (bottom); Mitchel Shenker: 167

Library of Congress Cataloging-in-Publication Data is available from the publisher
Printed in Korea by Sung In Printing

00 01 02 03 04 05 / 5 4 3 2 1